GT
PUBLISHING

By RICHARD SIMMONS

Editorial Development by David Ricketts
Art Direction and Design by Barbara Marks
Recipes by Richard Simmons and Winifred Morice
Photographs by Ed Ouellette

GT
PUBLISHING

RICHARD SIMMONS

FAREWELL TO FAT

HOMEMADE IN THE U.S.A.

COOKBOOK

David Ricketts, Editorial Development
Barbara Marks, Art Direction and Design
Beth Mackin, Production Director

Richard Simmons and Winifred Morice,
    Recipe Development
Lynda Hammersmith, Assistant
Recipe Testers:
Catherine Chatham
Susan Ehlich
Elaine Khosrova
Michael Krondl
Susan McQuillan
Sarah Reynolds

Ed Ouellette, Photographer
Melinda Wilson, First Assistant
Wolfgang Baeumle, Assistant
Johann Pieders, Assistant

Karen Gillingham, Food Stylist
Stormie Ingram, Assistant
Clément Bacqué, Assistant

Robin Tucker, Prop Stylist
Pat Eltiste, Assistant

Margery Tippie and Stephen R. Frankel,
    Copy Editors
Stephen R. Frankel, Proofreader
Patty Santelli, Nutritional Analysis
Toni Smith, Nutrirional Analysis

Leslie Wilshire, Richard Simmons wardrobe
Sheree Morgan, Richard Simmons makeup
Jimmy Grote, Richard Simmons hair

Erin Adams/Brainworks, painted backdrops

Test Kitchen provided by Claire and Joe
    Enfield

Published by GT Publishing Corporation
16 East 40th Street
New York, New York 10016

Library of Congress Catalog Card Number: 96-77555
ISBN: 1-57719-102-1

Manufactured in the United States of America

First Printing 1996

10 9 8 7 6 5 4 3 2 1

Contents

The People Who Make a Difference

This reminds me of the Oscars, acknowledging all the people who helped me with the cookbook. I'm halfway through the acceptance speech, thanking all the hundreds of people and tastebuds, and oh no!—the orchestra begins to play the theme song louder and louder. I'm out of time! So you'll forgive me if I don't mention all your first and last names here. You know you are my inspiration.

So having said that, here are the people who were at my side, from the beginning to the end, almost day and night, as I dreamed and wrote this book. (If I didn't mention *these* people, I would never be able to eat again!)

India has the Taj Mahal, but I have **Winifred Morice**—she is a wonder. Besides helping me develop all the recipes for this book, she fills my life with so many other things. Winifred has been my special friend for twelve years, and she's worked with me on every one of my cookbooks. What else can I tell you about Winifred—she's a motivational nutritionist from New Zealand, teaches classes on my Cruises to Lose, writes poetry, plays the accordion, lives on a houseboat like Doris Day, has seven thousand clothing ensembles by *Platinum,* with matching jewelry, is married to a wonderful man who throws a party every Friday for his employees, continues to keep off the fifty pounds she lost twenty-five years ago, and she's been . . . but that's another story. Winifred's special touch is in each and every recipe in this cookbook—it comes from her heart.

And then there's **David Ricketts,** the father of the book, who steered us in the right direction through all the eating and writing (I think he *was* a cookbook in a previous life). He's a soft-spoken mix of Robert Young in "Marcus Welby M.D." *and* "Father Knows Best," plus a sprinkling of Ward Cleaver from "Leave It to Beaver" (with just a little bit of "I Love Lucy" thrown in—probably more Ethel than Lucy).

Fred Astaire had his partner, and David has his—**Barbara Marks,** the crème brûlée of art directors, the Michelangelo of cookbook designers. She's made this book so beautiful that friends have framed it and hung it on their walls. Barbara to me is the best of Joan of Arc and Florence Nightingale—so passionate about her work, but caring enough to listen to all my crazy ideas. That's how we came up with the photo of the fork and me on the cover, and all those photos of me for the chapter openers. Barbara let me play, but one special look from her, and I knew I had gone off the deep end, even for me!

Ed Ouellette (pronounced wha-let) has captured my *pudum* on film for a decade—he's caught me sweatin', smilin', and cookin'. And his pictures of the food in this cookbook are so delicious that I've actually seen people licking the pages!

Karen Gillingham, the food stylist, and **Robin Tucker,** the prop stylist, created the beautiful canvases of food that Ed photographed.

With twenty-two years in the book business (yet still so boyishly preppie), **Tom Klusaritz,** Vice President of Publishing at GoodTimes, was the master chef who went shopping for the team. He combined us all in the same pot, stirred in the spices, and then let it happen—but kept an eye on the stove, making sure we were always simmering with wonderful aromas.

Also at GoodTimes Publishing, I can always count on **Andy Greenberg, Lynn Hamlin,** and **Karen Wolf** to listen to my ideas and help me make them real. They, together with my agents **Rick Bradley** and **Rick Hersh** at the William Morris Agency, are my dream team.

None of this would be possible without the **Cayre family** at GoodTimes. They've made me part of their family, and I'm proud of that.

In Los Angeles, there are all my friends I see or talk to every day, who help keep the hours organized, and do so much more:

Michael Catalano, the man with the fabulous eyebrows, is my manager who makes sure I know where I'm going each day, and that I get there—he's my compass.

Jimmy Grote has been doing my hair for eleven years—yes, it is my own hair—plus, he bakes a wonderful loaf of bread. You figure the connection; I can't. Oh, now you're thinking that my hair looks like a loaf of bread? Jimmy tasted all the recipes in this book, and made many, many suggestions. And if that isn't enough, he does a wicked crossword puzzle, in ink—so intelligent.

Marilyn has been part of my family for sixteen years. She's the person I can count on to tell me what she really thinks, about the recipes, the photographs, the book cover. We all have a *mensch* in our life, and Marilyn is mine.

Teresa is the woman who lives with me, taking care of me and my dogs. What would I do without her? She's an honest and beautiful woman.

Elijah Jones has worked with me for fourteen years and now lives in Hattiesburg, Mississippi, where he works out of his home on many of my projects, including my newsletter of which he's the Associate Editor. You may know Elijah from some of my aerobic tapes. He lost 295 pounds and has kept it off all these years.

Leslie Wilshire has been with me for a decade, designing and creating all my fabulous tank tops as well as other parts of my wardrobe. And **Sheree Morgan** makes me look more beautiful and younger than I really am (pushing 50!). They're my beauty girls.

I don't usually feed my three **dalmatians** table food, but I made an exception for some of the recipes from this book—I know what their favorites are. Thank you for being part of my life, girls.

And finally, a big thank you to **Shirley** my mom, **Leonard** my brother, and **Brent,** their most fabulous dalmatian, for letting me mess up the kitchen for the first sixteen years of my life.

So here we are—just you, me, and this wonderful collection of low-fat American recipes, homemade in the U.S.A. Many of us have been together before—in my exercise classes, on my cruises, and even on the telephone, talking about what you eat and how much you exercise. But for many of you, this is the first time we've met. Hi, how are you? Maybe you're already eating O.K. and you're just looking for some new low-fat recipes to add to your own collection. This book is for you, too. This book is for all of you. Let me explain.

First of all, let's get one thing straight—this is not a diet book. This is a book to help you start or improve a healthy lifestyle. About fourteen years ago I wrote a book called the *Never-Say-Diet Cookbook*. Those were the days when the word "diet" meant "Get rid of those pounds, honey!" Now "diet" more often than not means the food you put on the table every day, and that food may have nothing to do with losing weight. That's how wise man Webster defines it. So, now that we understand that, let's move on.

For years I've been traveling back and forth across America, probably about 400,000 miles a year. If you can remember when I was on the T.V. show "General Hospital" and the original "Richard Simmons Show," you can guess how long I've been traveling. (If you do figure it out, please don't tell anyone else!) As I've gone from city to city and mall to mall, helping people lose millions of pounds (collectively, that is), I've gathered together America's favorite recipes from all four corners of the map—delicious but, more often than not, full of fat.

Early one morning about a year and half ago, before the telephone started ringing, I was sitting quietly in my kitchen (I know, that's hard to believe, me sitting quietly). And I found myself thinking, Wouldn't it be great to create a cookbook with easy-to-prepare classic American recipes, and make them low-fat—

and include all the stories about where I found the recipes, together with a little American history, fun facts about ingredients, and all the other stuff that makes eating (and reading about food) the best pleasure in life. Well, one of the two best pleasures. I would include all those wonderful foods I ate while growing up in New Orleans, which to me is the culinary capital of the U.S., but I'd make the recipes low-fat, too. So into my kitchen I went, along with Winifred Morice, my longtime accomplice in policing the fat out of food, and we started banging the pots and pans.

And here it is—the cookbook I dreamed of. America's best recipes, with all the extra fat now sitting on my kitchen floor. And these are easy recipes you can make yourself, in your own kitchen.

As you leaf through this book looking at the pretty pictures, you'll notice that each recipe has a beautiful picture showing you how the finished dish will look and a nutrition analysis, including the percentage of fat calories. But more about that later.

TOO MUCH OF A GOOD THING

My favorite subject is food. I love it. I love the feel, smell, and taste of it. I like it hot, warm, and cold. I can eat when I'm happy, or sad—it makes no difference. I have a passion for food, and, in fact, I am a compulsive eater. In my case, I've learned the trick is to know when to put the fork down and walk away.

Over the years as I've traveled and taught classes at Slimmons, my exercise studio in Beverly Hills, I've identified six kinds of eaters who just overdo it, hotly pursuing different foods, and putting on the pounds. See if you recognize yourself. First, there are the **foodies.** They just love food—all of it, all the time. It doesn't make any difference what the food is; they just love it, and they can't get enough of it. That's me. Then there's the **buttering up** group—butter on bread, rolls, crackers, sandwiches, baked potatoes, vegetables, meat, cereal, and little crocks of the melted gold served with every meal for dunking or for applying directly to the tongue. **Just cheesy** is exactly what you think it is—cheese in every recipe: hamburgers, casseroles, dips, chocolate cheese, apple pie. You get the picture. Next, the **sweet jaw.** Not just a sweet tooth, but the whole jaw. These are the people who knew before anybody else that tiramisu was not a disease from Mexico. These are the same people who take vacations to Hershey Park in Pennsylvania rather than Disney World in Orlando. You know what the fastest-selling items are on the T.V. home shopping channels? Candy dishes. **It's a fried life!** These folks only know a potato as something fried—French fries, potato chips, fried potato skins. This is me also. Remember I told you I like food hot, warm, and cold? Well, I especially like it fried. And finally, there are the **shakers.** Just put a salt shaker in their hand and they're happy. It's hard to see their food with that pile of salt on top. You would think that Lot had just passed through the neighborhood.

So there you have it, the Holy Trinity—F.S.S. (imagine air leaking out of a tire): fat, sugar, and salt. To keep your meals healthy, you need to use them in moderation. You don't have to eliminate them altogether, unless your doctor tells you to. And in some cases, a little extra fat or sugar is O.K. It's what I call Sacred Fat, Sacred Sweet, and Sacred Salt. Sounds like a back-up group for Aretha Franklin, but more about that later.

FAT—IN YOUR FOOD AND AROUND YOUR WAIST

Let's start with fat in general—a subject very close to my heart. There's fat in our bodies, and we need it, at least a little of it. It keeps us warm in winter, along with sweaters, flannel shirts, long underwear, and down comforters. It provides energy and dissolves certain vitamins (A, D, E, and K), carrying them through the body. I'll bet you didn't know that. Well, maybe some of you did. We're becoming much smarter about how our bodies work and what we need to eat and not eat. In food, fat adds flavor and feels good in the mouth—but I know you all knew that!

So, if fat does so many good things, why not just eat more and more of it? Well, foods high in fat, especially saturated fat, have been linked to all kinds of diseases. Sorry—I don't mean to bring you down, but it's the truth. And I won't even dwell on the obvious—extra pounds can slow us down and drain our energy.

THE THREE FAT SISTERS

Poor Cinderella! She had to put up with those awful sisters. But her life wasn't so bad, with her beautiful tiny feet and size 4 dress (even if she *did* only have one dress). Let me introduce you to the Three Fat Sisters. I'm sure you've met before, but perhaps not formally. And you know, two of the sisters are really not all that bad.

Saturated fat: This is the bad sister. Watch out! It's what I call yellow fat—you know, like butter. You find saturated fat in animal foods (not food *for* animals, but food *from* animals) and in tropical oils (used for frying lots of snack foods), and in whole milk, cream, cheese, butter, meat, chicken, vegetable shortening—sound familiar? At room temperature saturated fat is usually solid, like a stick of butter. Too much of this fat leads to pounds of extra weight and has been linked to increased cholesterol levels—not good for a healthy ticker.

Polyunsaturated and **monounsaturated fats:** These are the good fats. It is O.K. to invite Ms. Poly and Ms. Mono over for dinner, but not every night of the week. All fats carry calories, and we need to think about those calories. **Polyunsaturated fat** is found in many foods, including vegetable oils such as sunflower, corn, soybean, and safflower. Some varieties of fatty fish, such as salmon, mackerel, and tuna, contain a particular type of polyunsaturated fat called Omega-3 (and you thought Omega-3 was a T.V. spinoff of "Babylon 9"!). **Monounsaturated fat** is also found in some oils, such as olive, canola, and peanut.

So why make these distinctions? Listen closely. Polyunsaturated and monounsaturated fats, when they replace saturated fat in your recipes and meals (such as using oil rather than butter, or serving salmon instead of filet mignon), may help to lower your blood cholesterol levels. What's cholesterol? An ugly, waxy, fatlike substance produced in all animals, including us humans. If you have too much cholesterol, it may build up on the insides of your blood vessels, making the vessel openings smaller and smaller, and you can imagine what happens after that. Shudder, shudder!

So, you may ask: "Since poly and mono are such good friends, why not drink eight glasses of olive oil (high in monounsaturated fat) every day, like water? Then I'll always be a step ahead of coronary disease." (There's that nasty word disease again.) Well, the answer is no. Remember, the Greeks learned it before anybody else: everything in moderation. A couple of tablespoons of oil a day is fine —more than that, and you may start putting on weight, since oil also carries quite a few calories.

I hope what you just read makes sense to you. If it seems a little hazy, go back and read it again. Or give me a call and I'll explain it to you.

SHOULD I ONLY EAT NO-FAT PRODUCTS?

So what does all this stuff about fat mean? Sometimes fat is good, sometimes it's bad. You shouldn't eliminate all fat from your eating and cooking—no, no, no! We need fat, for all the reasons I mentioned above. Remember? If you eliminate all foods with fat, you'll eliminate a lot of other nutrients that are very important to your body. And those nutrients do the best good for you when they enter your body inside food rather than inside a pill or other dietary supplements. Listen to Mother Nature.

So, what about all those low-fat and no-fat products? Read the product labels. Sometimes such fat-modified products have more calories than the full-fat versions. And if you're trying to control your weight, calories are something you want to keep a very close watch over. And then there's taste. Some of these reduced-fat and no-fat foods just don't taste good. I'm not going to mention any names, but you've probably already discovered the ones that are good and the ones that aren't. If not, invite the neighbors over for a tast-

ing—keep the amounts small, please (not the neighbors, the foods). For example, buy all the different kinds of sour cream or ricotta cheese (full-fat, reduced-fat, low-fat, sort of no-fat, and no-fat), and taste them side by side. Now you see why I said keep the amounts small. You may discover that it's more satisfying to have a smaller amount of a higher-fat product than to have more of the reduced-fat or no-fat version, which tastes awful and racks up calories.

I know that this is a lot of information to digest and remember, but it's important.

THE 30 PERCENT SOLUTION

Now, let's talk about how much fat is too much. The American Heart Association and some other important organizations recommend that you get no more than 30 percent of your total calories from fat. Fat packs about double the calories, gram for gram, compared to protein and carbohydrates. The key here is that the 30 percent applies to *all* the food you eat in a day or week. If you applied the 30 percent to each dish, you would have to eliminate such favorites as hamburgers, cheese, peanuts, and most desserts. Yuk! Life would be no fun—I'd be ready to go to that great aerobic studio in the sky, right now! If you learn to make trade-offs, and balance an occasional hamburger with a healthy, low-fat pasta salad, "oven-fried" chicken, or low-fat macaroni-and-cheese, you can afford to spend the fat savings on a hamburger. (You noticed I said an "occasional" hamburger, which does *not* mean that occasionally each day I will have a hamburger. No—maybe once a *week*. That's it!)

HIGHER MATH

How do you figure this 30 percent? Don't start hyperventilating yet. I wasn't a math star in school—I lettered in eating. I got through math classes by washing cars and clothes for the nuns, re-dazzling their habits with extra bleach. So, if *I* can understand this, *you* can too. I'll try to explain it all as simply as possible. A calculator may help—and I know you have one of those, since none of us can do arithmetic anymore.

Here we go. Say you're taking in 2,000 calories

a day. Multiply the total calories by 0.30 (30 percent) to get the allowable calories from fat. Then divide the calories from fat by 9 (1 gram of fat = 9 calories) to get the allowable grams of fat per day. Wait, wait—don't throw your hands up yet. Follow this example:

2,000 (calories per day) x 0.30
= 600 (calories from fat)
600 divided by 9 (calories per gram of fat)
= 67 grams of fat

So, no more than 67 grams of fat per day, and hopefully even less. The 30 percent solution is meant to be a guideline for your *overall* eating, not a magnifying glass to make you paranoid every time you put something in your mouth. Eating should be fun—remember that. Didn't we start out talking about Sacred Fat a while back. Hold on, we'll get there eventually.

Back to 30 percent. Sometimes it *is* useful to look at an individual recipe and analyze it to see how it fits into your overall eating plan. Look at my Once-in-a-Blue-Moon Cheeseburger (page 56). Whoa! Wait a second. Forty percent calories from fat. What happened to the 30 percent solution? Isn't this supposed to be a low-fat cookbook? Yes, it is. But sit down. Here comes a nutrition lesson. Make a menu around this hamburger, adding a salad, plus fresh fruit for dessert, and the percentage will drop. Get the picture? It's the overall picture, not just the close-up—thank you, Mr. De Mille. Look at your numbers for the day, or even for the week. And if you go slightly over the 30 percent line once in a while, be easy on yourself. Just pull back on the next meal.

Here's one more math lesson. To figure out the percentage of calories of fat for an individual recipe, first multiply the grams of fat by 9 (9 calories per gram of fat) which will give you the total number of calories from fat. Then divide that number by the number of calories in the recipe, and that will give you the percentage. So for my blue cheese hamburger, it goes something like this:

16 grams fat x 9 (calories per gram of fat)
= 144 calories from fat
144 divided by 362 calories
= 40% calories from fat

SACRED FAT

You ready? Here's my concept of Sacred Fat. But first back up a moment. Remember I said that eating should be fun? If you've been eating healthy—you know, keeping an eye on calories and fat—then every now and then you can make a deliberate, conscious decision to have a little fat—Sacred Fat. And it should look like fat. Some of my favorites are butter, cheese, nuts, heavy cream, ice cream—stop me, stop me! My hamburger has two Sacred Fats—ground beef and blue cheese. Yum. It's certainly possible to lower the amount of fat in the burger by making it with ground turkey. But you know, sometimes you just want ground beef. You can't constantly deprive yourself of all the things you like. Life is too short. Just don't overdo it all the time, and when you do, overdo it sensibly.

Most of the recipes in this book weigh in at less than 30 percent calories from fat. But when they go over that limit, I'll point out the Sacred Fat I'm using.

Before you leave the room for a bathroom break, here's one more nutrition lesson. Always look at the number of grams of fat in a food item or recipe, as well as the percentage of calories from fat. Consider my Caesar, Mississippi, Salad (page 84). Forty-five percent calories from fat. Yikes! But take a closer look: only 7 grams of fat and 145 calories. When the calories are low, chances are the percentage will be misleadingly high. Remember, always take a look at the number of grams of fat.

SACRED SWEET

The same principle (not as in Victoria) applies here as with our friend Sacred Fat. Although excessive sugar—you know, treats such as candy bars, doughnuts, ice cream—adds calories and pounds, a little Sacred Sugar now and then adds fun flavor and tickles the sweet tooth—but make sure it doesn't rock the whole sweet jaw. A little molasses, honey, and even candied ginger can make you feel less deprived. And remember what Socrates said: "Moderation!"

SACRED SALT

When I was growing up in New Orleans, we salted everything. After we said grace at the dinner table, we all hollered, "Pass the salt!" During those days, I dreamed about that blue box of salt with the pretty girl and her umbrella. I thought everybody dumped heaps of salt onto gravy, tomatoes, corn on the cob, and watermelon. To this day, I still can't eat watermelon without salt, but now it's just a sprinkle.

A little salt lightly sprinkled—notice I said lightly—over cooked fresh foods brings out flavor, making food brighter. The problem is that so many of the foods we eat already come with salt built in: frozen entrees, canned string beans, chips, and on and on—you know the kinds of foods I'm talking about. Even though there are reduced-sodium and no-salt-added versions, there is still a lot of salt out there.

Sacred Salt is that salt you add to a dish to enhance its flavor—usually just a pinch, and if more, certainly try to keep it less than a ¼ teaspoon. Just a ¼ teaspoon of salt contains 533 milligrams of sodium; 1 teaspoon equals 2,131 milligrams of sodium. Some dishes, such as pasta and potatoes, will soak up the salt, so you may use a little more than usual with them. And some dishes are salt's natural partners—the corn on the cob and the tomatoes I mentioned before, for example.

Sacred Salt also hides in secret places: peanut butter, cheese, and canned tomato soup, for instance (the peanut butter and the cheese are also Sacred Fats). When you use these ingredients, cut back on the added salt.

NUTRITION INFORMATION

Each recipe in this book is followed by a nutrition breakdown for calories, protein, fat (including the percentage of calories from fat), and the amounts of carbohydrate, cholesterol, and sodium. The following chart gives you an idea of what your limits should be.

DAILY NUTRITION CHART

Refer to the nutritive content listings in my recipes, then use these guidelines to check that *daily* menus are well balanced and healthful.

Average Healthy Adult (Age 25+)		
	Women	Men
Calories[1]	2,000	2,700
Protein[2]	50 g (200 cal)	63 g (252 cal)
Fat[3]	66 g (594 cal)	90 g (810 cal)
Sodium[4]	1,100–3,300 mg	1,100–3,300 mg
Cholesterol[5]	300 mg	300 mg

[1]RDA [2](8%–12% of calories) RDA [3](30% of calories) American Heart Association and National Academy of Science [4]USDA [5]American Heart Association.

Calories (cal) that do not come from protein or fat should be derived from complex carbohydrates found in whole grains, fresh fruits, vegetables, pasta, etc.

PORTION PATROL

One of the keys to sane eating is portion control. If a recipe makes four servings, please don't eat the entire recipe yourself and say it's just one serving—that's more than a white lie, that's a fat lie.

And don't eyeball amounts when you're cooking—we all have different-size eyeballs. Measure, measure, measure. Don't trust your own judgment, especially if you're hungry. You need the proper equipment for measuring: measuring spoons, cups, and a scale. Don't be frightened by measuring or measuring equipment. Once you get used to them, it will all become second nature to you.

If a recipe calls for a 3-ounce boneless, skinned chicken breast, don't lift it up on your hand and say, "Yep, that feels like 3 ounces." Weigh it on a scale. For liquid ingredients, use a clear glass or plastic measuring cup with a pouring spout. To get the most accurate measure,

Weigh that food!

Measure, measure, measure!

No, my next Cruise to Lose is not down the Nile. What I'm talking about here is the Food Pyramid. No, don't get excited—it's not a pyramid-shaped gift box full of chocolate. In 1991, the United States Department of Agriculture (U.S.D.A.) along with some other folks developed the pyramid to show you how to eat (as if you didn't know already). We need more grains, vegetables, and fruits—those are all the foods at the base or foundation of the pyramid. And we need less meat, dairy products, and fats—they're at the top. The key to all this is the amount of servings per day. The actual serving sizes are probably smaller than what you're used to, especially if you think a Whopper a day will keep the doctor away. You also need to spread the required servings over more than one meal, since it's pretty difficult to have eleven servings of bread, cereal, rice, or pasta at one meal. If you can do that at one meal, your sense of portion control is really out of control.

place the cup on a flat surface and get your head down until your eye is level with the top of the liquid. You may even have to bend—good exercise.

For measuring dry ingredients, use a dry cup measure. These are usually made out of metal or plastic, and come in ⅓, ¼, ½, and 1 cup sizes. Spoon or pour the dry ingredient into the measuring cup, and sweep away the excess with a chopstick or the blunt straight edge of a knife to level the top. If you're measuring flour, lightly spoon it into the measuring cup and use the same method to level the top.

For small quantities of both dry and liquid ingredients, use measuring spoons.

Compare sizes so that you know what large, medium, and small mean—for instance, a large apple, a medium shrimp, a small potato. Small is not large, and large is not small. Got it?

For more about other kitchen equipment, see pages 16 and 17.

Now, let's get back to what we were discussing before our little diversion about equipment. We were talking about portion control, and that leads us to the pyramid.

FOOD GUIDE PYRAMID
A Guide to Daily Food Choices

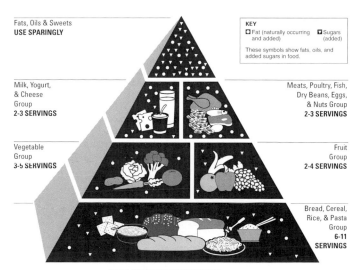

Source: U.S. Department of Agriculture &
U.S. Department of Health and Human Services

Here are some examples of single-serving sizes:

BREAD, CEREAL, RICE, AND PASTA (6–11 SERVINGS)
1 slice of bread; ½ bagel; ½ English muffin;
1 ounce ready-to-eat cereal; ½ cup cooked rice
or pasta; 1 pancake

VEGETABLES (3–5 SERVINGS)
1 cup raw leafy vegetables; ½ cup vegetables,
cooked or chopped raw; ½ cup compact salads;
¾ cup vegetable juice

FRUITS (2–4 SERVINGS)
1 medium apple, banana, orange, kiwi, pear, or
peach; ½ cup canned, chopped fresh, or cooked
fruit; ¼ cup dried fruit; ¾ cup fruit juice

MILK, YOGURT, AND CHEESE (2–3 SERVINGS)
*Here it makes sense to avoid the high-fat products, and
instead use nonfat or low-fat (1%) milk, nonfat yogurt,
and part-skim, reduced-fat, or nonfat cheeses.*
1 cup milk or yogurt; 1½ ounces natural cheese

**MEAT, POULTRY, SEAFOOD, DRY BEANS, EGGS, AND
NUTS (2–3 SERVINGS)**
2 to 3 ounces cooked lean meat, poultry (without
the skin is even better), or fish; ½ cup cooked
dry beans; 4 to 6 tablespoons peanut butter;
2 to 3 eggs (because egg yolks are high in cholesterol, try to limit your egg basket to no more than
4 per week)

FATS, OILS, AND SWEETS (USE SPARINGLY)

WHAT'S IT ALL ABOUT: LABELS

Now you're ready for the ultimate test: shopping. But
first a suggestion. If you wear reading glasses, take
them to the supermarket. Even a magnifying glass
will help. Notice all those traffic jams in the grocery
aisles these days—it's people huddled together, reading labels. You may even meet a label pal.

Guess what? The nutrition panel on most packaged foods these days now includes the number of
grams of total fat plus saturated fat and the number of
milligrams of cholesterol per serving of food. The
Percent Daily Value ("% Daily Value") on the label is a
guide for measuring the amount of certain nutrients
in a serving against your overall needs.

Now take a look at the front of the label. What
do all those words mean: fat-free, low-fat, reduced-
fat, lite, cholesterol-free, and on and on. Well, I'm
here to tell all!

fat-free: less than 0.5 grams of fat per serving
low-fat: 3 grams of fat or less per serving
reduced-fat, less fat: at least 25 percent less fat
per serving when compared with a similar food
cholesterol-free: less than 2 milligrams of cholesterol per serving, and 2 grams or less of saturated fat per serving
low cholesterol: 20 milligrams or less of cholesterol per serving, and 2 grams or less of saturated
fat per serving
lean: packaged meat, poultry, or seafood that when
cooked has less than 10 grams of total fat, less
than 4 grams of saturated fat, and less than 95
milligrams of cholesterol per serving
extra lean: packaged meat, poultry, or seafood
that when cooked has less than 5 grams of total
fat, less than 2 grams of saturated fat, and less
than 95 milligrams of cholesterol per serving
light or lite: at least one-third fewer calories or
50 percent less fat than a regular serving. If more
than half the calories are from fat, the fat content
must be reduced by 50 percent or more.

Now, can you remember all that? If not, take notes on
a little piece of paper and smuggle it into the supermarket. You're ready!

No, wait a second, here are a few more suggestions. To make short work of shopping, try to plan
your menus in advance. Gather the recipes together,
take a look at what you already have in the house, and
then make a shopping list according to how foods are
arranged in your supermarket—it's your map to better eating. And do you remember that wise old say-
ing, "An army travels on its stomach"? Well, make
sure yours is full before you go shopping. You don't
want to arrive at the checkout line with a shopping
cart full of empty wrappers and boxes! And filling up

before you shop doesn't mean you have to chow down—a glass or two of water will do it!

Which reminds me—are you drinking enough water a day? Eight glasses? Good. I thought you were. Water is like the mailman and garbage collector combined. Water helps deliver the good things to all parts of the body and takes away the bad things, plus it's good for the skin. And we all want to keep that young, dewy look.

FLAVOR

Food has to taste good. I don't care what kind of eating plan you're following. Nothing will work unless the food tastes good. We all know that fat makes things taste good. If we eliminate the fat, then we have to add flavor from somewhere else.

You've heard that expression "Put a little spice in your life"? Let me introduce you to fresh herbs—your flavor friends. Get used to keeping them around. Just a little bit added to foods will make all the difference. It's usually best to add fresh herbs to hot dishes toward the end of the cooking, since their flavor will fade with too much heat. And, oh, to store them, here are a few tips: Wash them gently and make sure to shake off all the excess moisture; wrap them in paper towels and refrigerate. Basil and mint, however, are special and need to be treated differently—if they get damp, they'll turn black. So, store these herbs in the refrigerator, unwashed and upright with their stems in a jar of water, just like a bouquet, covered loosely with a plastic bag.

basil: Reminds me of a blend of licorice, clove, and tarragon. This herb was created especially for tomatoes—fresh tomatoes, tomato sauce, tomato soup, casseroles with tomatoes, and so on. A little sprig also makes a colorful garnish.

chives: And you thought these were just lawn clippings. Part of the onion family, chives add a delicate flavor to dishes. Just take a kitchen shears and snip them directly into the dish. Add to soups, salads, pasta dishes, vegetables, fish, poultry, or whatever. When chives bloom, they have a beautiful purple blossom on the end that makes a great garnish.

cilantro (a.k.a. **Chinese parsley** or **coriander**): This looks like a smaller version of parsley, but the edges are saw-toothed. And it sure doesn't taste like parsley. Cilantro has a very distinctive taste, almost like eating a menthol candy. It's what gives much Southwest and Mexican cooking and some Asian cooking their distinctive flavor.

dill: Dill mayonnaise—one of my favorites. But make sure it's reduced-fat mayo. The lemony-fresh flavor of dill is good in potato salad, salad dressings, with fish, and in yogurt-based dips, and excellent in chicken dishes.

mint: Mint juleps and mint jelly! Use whole leaves to garnish desserts, or chop it up and add it to fruit salads (or to any salad), and to sauces, rice, and cooked vegetables.

oregano: Oregano is a multiple-personality herb (actually in the mint family). Depending on the variety, it can be mild or very peppery. Snitch a small leaf while you're shopping (make sure that no one is watching) and see what it tastes like. What's a pizza or tomato sauce without this herb? Also good in stews, bean dishes, vegetable salads, and cooked vegetables.

parsley: This is more than just a piece of lawn clipping you put on the side of the plate for a garnish. Chop some up and throw it into dishes to add a wonderful fresh green taste. And it comes in two varieties: the frilly leaf that you probably already know, and the flat-leaf Italian, which is a little stronger than the frilly. (Isn't that true of all Italians?) Toss a handful of chopped parsley into salads, including potato and macaroni, and into steamed vegetables, tomato sauces, and soups—almost any dish gets a lift from this fresh bit of green.

rosemary: Sun-warmed pine needles— that's what this smells like. Imparts wonderful flavor to most meats, especially lamb, and adds a note of mystery to vegetable side dishes.

sage: Strong but pleasant flavor. Good with poultry, pork, and dried bean dishes.

thyme: This tastes like a collision between lemon and mint! Sprinkle over fish dishes, including chowders, and add to poultry recipes, beef stew, tomato sauces, and rice dishes.

freshly ground black pepper: You can buy little jars (or even big jars) of already ground black pepper. But after it sits around for a bit, the flavor fades. Better to invest in a good pepper mill—you won't have to skip a mortgage payment to afford one—and then buy whole black peppercorns and load them into the mill. Then grind the pepper when you need it, just the way they do in restaurants with those three-foot-long pepper mills. Try the white peppercorns, too—they're a little milder than the black and won't add black specks if you're seasoning an all-white dish. There are also blends of peppercorns that include a mix of several different colors. If a recipe calls for a large measurement, grind the pepper onto a small piece of wax paper and then pour it into the measuring spoon rather than trying to grind it directly into the tiny area of the spoon.

citrus zest: Who ever invented zest deserves a place in heaven! The zest is the outermost layer of the colored part of the peel, and it contains highly flavored citrus oils. I use lemon zest a lot in my recipes—it makes food perky (like you-know-who). What's the best way to get the zest off a lemon or lime or orange? The trick is to avoid the white layer under the thin skin—it has a bitter taste. There's a tool called a zester (the one with the red handle). Lightly scrape it across the skin of the lemon and you'll get gorgeous curly yellow strands. Use these as a garnish, or chop them up and add them to a dish. You say you don't have a zester? Then take a swivel-bladed vegetable peeler and remove thin strips of the peel (remember, avoid the bitter white layer). You can slice the strips into thin pieces for garnish, or chop away.

And speaking of zesting, here are some simple pieces of kitchen equipment that are really important:

A kitchen timer is essential. Don't trust a wall clock or wristwatch. When I get on the telephone, I forget about the time. You probably do, too. So get a timer that's easy to read and has a buzzer or chime as loud as Big Ben.

An oven thermometer—you can't live without it. Most ovens are least 25° off—too hot or too cold. So just keep that thermometer in there all the time, and your cooking should become even more perfect!

Pots and pans? Just a few. You don't need enough to outfit a wagon train heading west: a **small, medium,** and **large skillet with a good non-stick surface** (cuts down on the amount of fat or cooking spray you need), and **the same for saucepans.** A 6-quart **Dutch oven** is not a bad idea, either.

And there you have it.

Now that we've covered the basic equipment, here are some basic techniques. School's not out yet.

Speaking of thermometers, **an instant-read meat thermometer** is an excellent investment and only costs about $7 or $8. It's great for quickly checking the internal temperature of chicken, a beef roast, and, of course, that holiday turkey. When you serve roast chicken to guests, you'll be certain you won't surprise them with chicken sushi instead.

For **knives,** you really only need three: **small, medium,** and **long.** The small one, or **paring knife,** is just a few inches long and is ideal for the small jobs: peeling a tomato, hulling strawberries, slicing one carrot, trimming green onions, and (my personal favorite) sculpting radish roses—you get the picture. The medium or **chef's knife** comes in a couple of different sizes—I like the 8-inch one. Anything longer, and I feel like Bruce Lee. This knife is great for everything: chopping, dicing, and slicing, and the side can be used for crushing cloves of garlic. The long thin **carver** is used for thinly slicing roasts, bread, tomatoes, and for carving poultry.

The **swivel-bladed vegetable peeler** needs no introduction. But look for the newer model with an oversize cushy rubber handle—it's much more comfortable than the old-fashioned metal-handled variety, and very easy to use if you have a touch of stiffness in the wrists.

HOW TO DICE

No, this is not rolling for snake-eyes. Dicing is like chopping, but not as willy-nilly. Your goal is to cut almost square pieces that are all the same size, about ¼ to ½ inch.

1. To dice a vegetable, first slice the vegetable vertically with several evenly spaced cuts. Don't cut all the way through the end, and hold the vegetable so it keeps its original shape.

2. Then, slice the vegetable with evenly spaced horizontal cuts. (With an onion you really don't need to do this, since the vegetable is already naturally separated into rings).

3. Now, just slice down vertically at right angles to the first set of vertical cuts, and you'll have instant diced pieces. This is one of those cases where a picture is worth a thousand words— well, at least thirty or so.

HOW TO JULIENNE?

This is not a square-dance step. Julienning is cutting food into thin strips or matchsticks. First, cut the food (here, a zucchini—but the same would apply to carrots, eggplant, potatoes, etc.) into horizontal slices. Then stack the slices, and cut them into the size strips or sticks you want. And as you can probably figure out from the picture, if you cut the sticks crosswise, you end up dicing your vegetable!

SKIN THAT TOMATO, AND SEED IT WHILE YOU'RE AT IT!

Tomato seeds and skins can be so unsightly when they are floating about in a dish. Also, sometimes you may just want the meaty part of the tomato without all the extra juice. Here's how to do it: Lower the tomatoes into a pot of boiling water for about thirty seconds. Then plunge them into an ice water bath to prevent them from cooking and getting mushy. Using a paring knife and working over a bowl to catch any juices, peel off the skin. Next, cut the tomatoes in half crosswise. Working over the bowl again, scoop out the pulp and seeds with the tip of a spoon or a clean fingertip. If you want, save the juices and pulp to add to soup or sauces. And now, the tomatoes are ready to chop or slice or whatever.

PETER PEPPER, ROAST THAT PEPPER.

I love roasted peppers—they have such a yummy sweet, smoky flavor. They're delicious in salads, soups, stews, and even sandwiches. You can buy them in jars, but I like to roast them myself. And it's so simple to do: Put the peppers under a broiler or on an outdoor grill, turning them frequently, until the skin is blackened all over. Then pop them while still hot into a brown paper bag and close the bag. Let them sit there for about fifteen minutes. Take them out and, with a paring knife, peel off the skin. Core and seed them and you're ready to go.

THE BOTTOM LINE

So now I've taken you through it all: the Three Fat Sisters, the pros and cons of eating gobs and gobs of fat-free products, the 30 percent solution, Sacred F.S.S., the Pyramid, cooking equipment, how to get extra flavor in your food, and so on. Whew! That was a lot. But the most important lesson is the easiest to remember. Food is your very special friend, not your enemy. Learn to love, cherish, and enjoy it. And as in all friendships, there must be respect—respect for yourself, for the food, and for your friendship with food. (But let me tell you, it's O.K. to do a little overindulging now and then—mostly then—as long as you stay close to the straight and narrow.) One other thing: never sacrifice taste. What's life without wonderful-tasting food? With it, it's an affair to remember!

Fired-Up Buffalo "Wings"

Prep: 5 minutes
Marinate: 30 to 60 minutes
Bake: 425° for 20 minutes

Want to hear a real story about American ingenuity? Late one night at the Anchor Bar in Buffalo, New York, Dominick Bellissimo asked his mom, Teressa, the cook and co-owner of this restaurant-bar, to cook up a midnight snack for him and his buddies. The only thing Teressa had on hand was a pile of chicken wings set aside for soup stock. But Mom loved her son Dominick, so she said what the heck. No soup! She cooked the wings in some hot oil, brushed them with a tangy barbecue sauce, and served them with a blue cheese dressing and celery sticks—the rest is history. Thank you, Teressa!

1 pound chicken drumettes
¼ cup hot pepper sauce
1 tablespoon Worcestershire sauce
2 teaspoons paprika
⅛ teaspoon cayenne, or less for milder flavor
1 cup fat-free blue cheese–flavored salad dressing
8 celery sticks

1 In sealable plastic bag combine drumettes, hot pepper sauce, Worcestershire sauce, 1 teaspoon paprika, and cayenne. Seal bag and shake to coat chicken. Refrigerate and marinate at least 30 minutes.

2 Preheat oven to 425°. Remove drumettes from marinade and arrange in single layer in shallow baking pan. Sprinkle with half the remaining paprika.

3 Bake 10 minutes. Turn drumettes over. Sprinkle with remaining paprika. Bake another 10 minutes or until meat is no longer pink near bone.

4 Pour blue cheese dressing into small bowl. Arrange chicken and celery sticks on serving platter. Accompany with blue cheese dressing for dipping.

Sacred Fat

What are Buffalo wings without the skin? I make the choice here to keep the Sacred Fat skin on, although you could remove it before marinating for an even skinnier version—but they won't taste as good. Even with the skin on, the fat checks in at only 6 grams per serving. But promise you won't eat more than your portion—one recipe is not one serving, it's four!

NUTRIENT VALUE PER SERVING
206 calories   18 g protein
6 g fat (29% fat)   17 g carbohydrate
755 mg sodium   51 mg cholesterol

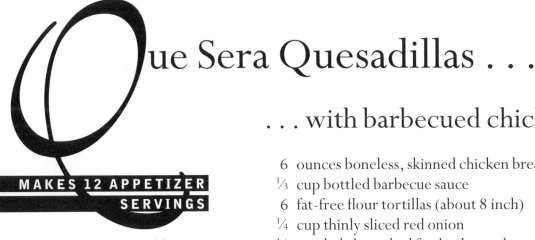

Que Sera Quesadillas . . .

. . . with barbecued chicken

Prep: 10 minutes
Broil: 4 minutes
Cook: 6 minutes

My love of barbecue grew from a wonderful memory of a small BBQ chicken restaurant just outside of Dallas. I can still remember bowls of extra barbecue sauce on the table. When no one was looking, I stuck in my finger and snuck a quick taste—I was hooked. So now you see why I couldn't pass up the chance to sneak some barbecue sauce into my chicken quesadilla. To me, a quesadilla makes the perfect lunch, or even snack—it's a cross between a sandwich and a pizza. Whatever will be, will be.

6 ounces boneless, skinned chicken breasts
⅓ cup bottled barbecue sauce
6 fat-free flour tortillas (about 8 inch)
¼ cup thinly sliced red onion
¼ cup lightly packed fresh cilantro leaves
6 canned pitted black olives, sliced, *or* ¼ avocado, pitted, peeled, and chopped
⅔ cup shredded reduced-fat Monterey Jack cheese
Nonstick vegetable oil cooking spray

1 Preheat broiler. Place chicken on rack in broiler pan. Spread with some of barbecue sauce.

2 Broil 1 to 2 inches from heat for 2 minutes. Turn chicken over. Spread with more barbecue sauce. Broil 1 to 2 minutes more or until meat is no longer pink in center. Cut chicken into bite-size chunks.

3 Place tortillas on flat surface. Spread with remaining barbecue sauce. Scatter chicken chunks over half of each tortilla. Top with red onion, a few cilantro leaves, olives or avocado, and cheese. Fold over each tortilla in half to enclose filling.

4 Coat large nonstick skillet with cooking spray. Heat over medium-high heat. Place 2 quesadillas at a time in skillet. Cook until lightly browned and cheese is melted, about 1 minute each side. To serve, cut each quesadilla in half.

NUTRIENT VALUE PER SERVING
101 calories   7 g protein
2 g fat (20% fat)   14 g carbohydrate
212 mg sodium   13 mg cholesterol

. . . with vegetables

Nonstick vegetable oil cooking spray
- 2 cups sliced (¼ inch thick) vegetables such as eggplant, bell peppers, zucchini, and yellow squash
- 6 fat-free flour tortillas (about 8 inch)
- 2 to 3 tablespoons chopped fresh cilantro
- 1 cup shredded part-skim mozzarella cheese
- ½ cup bottled medium-hot salsa *or* Hatch, New Mexico, Fresh Tomato Salsa (page 34)

1 Preheat broiler. Coat baking pan with cooking spray. Arrange vegetable slices in single layer in pan, placing peppers skin side up. Coat vegetables lightly with cooking spray.

2 Broil vegetables about 2 inches from heat for 10 minutes or until browned, turning all once, except peppers. Remove vegetables and let cool. Peel peppers.

3 Place 3 tortillas on flat surface. Divide vegetables over each. Top with cilantro, cheese, and salsa. Cover with remaining tortillas.

4 Coat nonstick skillet with cooking spray. Heat over medium-high heat. Place quesadillas one at a time in skillet, and cook until lightly browned and cheese is melted, about 1 minute on each side.

5 Cut each quesadilla into 4 wedges. Serve immediately.

MAKES 12 APPETIZER SERVINGS

Prep: 10 minutes
Broil: 10 minutes
Cook: 6 minutes

I like to slice vegetables such as zucchini and eggplant lengthwise so that the pieces will be large. If I'm grilling the vegetables, this works especially well, since there's less chance of the pieces slipping through the grill rack. How embarrassing — it's happened to me!

NUTRIENT VALUE PER SERVING
89 calories   4 g protein
2 g fat (17% fat)   14 g carbohydrate
234 mg sodium   5 mg cholesterol

# Honey, I Shrunk the Ham and Cheese Sandwiches

MAKES 24 APPETIZER SERVINGS

Prep: 15 minutes
Bake: 375° for 10 to 12 minutes

I like having little statues of pigs around because they're a symbol of good luck and prosperity. Have one of these mini-sandwiches and your appetite will be blessed with good fortune. Have several, and you'd best stay away from the scale. If making these for a party, just multiply the ingredient amounts by 1½ (for 36 servings) or 2 (for 48 servings), figuring one per person, or maybe two. These are also delicious with soup instead of the usual fat-laden buttery crackers.

Nonstick vegetable oil cooking spray
All-purpose flour, for rolling
12 pieces (1 ounce *each*) frozen bread roll dough *or* frozen bread dough, thawed
Dijon-style mustard (optional)
12 extra-thin slices Black Forest ham (about 3 ounces)
12 thin slices reduced-fat cheese such as cheddar or Monterey Jack (about 2 ounces)
Sesame seeds (optional)

1 Preheat oven to 375°. Coat nonstick baking sheet with cooking spray. On lightly floured board, using floured rolling pin, roll each piece of dough out to a 3½ x 3½-inch square. If desired, spread each with a little mustard.

2 On top of each dough square, place 1 slice ham and 1 slice cheese, folded to fit neatly. Roll up dough to enclose filling. Cut in half and trim edges if necessary. Roll in sesame seeds if desired. Place, seam side down and 1 inch apart, on prepared baking sheet.

3 Bake 10 to 12 minutes or until heated through and dough is golden brown.

Bread Dough is one of those products you can use in lots of different ways. Look for it in the refrigerator section or frozen food section of your supermarket. If you can't find the dough for rolls, often called Parker House rolls (after the famous hotel in Boston), buy a loaf of frozen bread dough and tear off 1-ounce portions.

NUTRIENT VALUE PER SERVING
51 calories   4 g protein
1 g fat (16% fat)   7 g carbohydrate
248 mg sodium   3 mg cholesterol

Which Ham Should I Use?

Ham is one of those foods I consider to be Sacred Fat. It has so much flavor that a little goes a long way. In this sandwich, just a very skinny slice will do ya'—0.3 g fat per very thin slice.

Here's a list of different hams you can use in your roll-ups. Even though this book is a collection of American recipes, I've included some imported hams because of their wonderful flavor.

Black Forest ham—A heavily smoked ham from Germany; very good with sourdough or a dark bread.

Boiled ham—Everybody knows this one. Not as much flavor as other varieties.

Country hams—These traditionally come from our southeastern states. The most famous is Smithfield, which comes from proper pigs who live in Smithfield, Virginia, and are fed a diet of peanuts. This ham is very, very salty, so you need to soak it first. For these sandwiches, I use just a thin sliver of this ham.

Prosciutto—Dry-cured (not smoked) with allspice, nutmeg, coriander, and mustard, this ham comes from Parma, Italy, but a version is now produced in the U.S.A. These pigs are fed chestnuts.

Virginia ham—A fully cooked boneless ham, usually smoked over hickory and applewood, sometimes glazed and studded with cloves. Peanuts and acorns are the diet here.

Westphalian ham—A rich German ham, smoked over beechwood with juniper berries thrown in for good measure (juniper is used to make gin!). The pigs are fed beets!

You-Can-Have-Only-One Stuffed Mushroom

MAKES 12 APPETIZER SERVINGS

Prep: 15 minutes
Cook: 2 minutes
Bake: 375° for 15 minutes

I tasted my first stuffed mushroom at a wedding reception. It was so delicious I said to the waiter, "Give me the platter and I'll serve them for you." Well, by the time I got to the first guest, the mushrooms were gone! Now whenever I go to a wedding reception (or *any* reception) I ask, "Are you serving stuffed mushrooms? Oh you are! Well I'll be happy to pass the platter for you."

NUTRIENT VALUE PER SERVING
26 calories   2 g protein
1 g fat (39% fat)   2 g carbohydrate
100 mg sodium   3 mg cholesterol

12 large whole white mushrooms

Nonstick olive oil cooking spray

¼ cup *each* grated Parmesan cheese *and* low-fat ricotta cheese

2 tablespoons *each* chopped fresh parsley *and* fresh bread crumbs

1 teaspoon *each* fresh lemon juice *and* minced garlic

¼ teaspoon salt

⅛ teaspoon freshly ground black pepper

1 Preheat oven to 375°. Wipe mushrooms clean with damp paper towel. Twist and pull out stems, leaving cavity for stuffing. Set mushrooms aside, cavity side up. Trim ends from stems. Finely dice stems. Coat small nonstick skillet with cooking spray and heat over medium-high heat. Add diced mushroom stems. Cook, stirring, over medium-high heat for 2 minutes or until lightly browned.

2 In small bowl mix remaining ingredients. Add browned mushroom stems and stir to mix thoroughly.

3 Spoon stuffing mixture into upturned mushroom caps. Arrange in small baking pan.

4 Bake, uncovered, 15 minutes or until mushrooms are cooked and heated through.

Looks Like a Lot of Fat, But It Isn't.

At first glance these look like a fat no-no. (Remember, you're only having one of these; okay, maybe two if no one is looking, but that's it!) The percentage of calories from fat is 39 percent—that's high. But there's only 1 gram of fat per mushroom—much less than most low-fat cookies or chips, or even vegetable side dishes tossed with a little sauce. The calories are very low, too: 25 per mushroom. Figure it out yet? Since the calories are low, the ratio of grams of fat to calories is high, even though the mushroom itself is a fairly "healthy" morsel. The lesson here? Don't stop with just the percentage of calories from fat; also take a look at how many grams of fat and calories a particular food has.

ini Ha-Ha Pizzas

Prep: 20 minutes
Bake: 500° for 8 minutes
per baking sheet

Did you know that we eat about 90 acres of pizza a day — not just me, but all of us together? That's a lot of crust. Pizza has become a very American thing — I'm surprised we haven't seen a McPizza yet. My pizzas here are small ones — they're so cute and happy-looking, they'll make you smile. Have a couple of these, along with a green salad (easy on the dressing), and you've got lunch.

8 pieces (1 ounce *each*) frozen bread roll dough *or* bread dough, thawed
All-purpose flour, for rolling
Nonstick olive oil cooking spray
½ cup pasta-ready tomato sauce
2 ounces turkey link sausage, frozen and partially thawed
½ cup sliced fresh mushrooms
¼ cup chopped onion *or* green onion (white and green parts)
½ cup shredded part-skim mozzarella cheese

1 Preheat oven to 500°. Shape thawed bread dough into balls. On floured board, using rolling pin, roll out to 3- or 4-inch circles, or pat out with your hands. Coat 2 baking sheets with cooking spray. Place 4 circles of dough on each sheet. Spread each circle with 1 tablespoon sauce.

2 With sharp knife, slice partially thawed sausage into very thin slices. Divide sausage slices, sliced mushrooms, and chopped onion equally over dough circles. Sprinkle with cheese.

3 Bake, one tray at a time, about 8 minutes or until crusts are browned and cheese is melted. Let cool slightly. Remove to wooden board. Slice each pizza into 4 wedges.

NUTRIENT VALUE PER SERVING
27 calories   2 g protein
1 g fat (27% fat)   4 g carbohydrate
76 mg sodium   2 mg cholesterol

Tops and Bottoms

We've come a long way since that first tomato pizza in Naples. Use my topping here just as a starting point. Other variations pictured include a simple sliced tomato with shredded part-skim mozzarella and fresh basil leaves to a more fancy artichoke heart and sun-dried tomato. The sky really is the limit. I've actually seen a ham pizza with pineapple rings on top—the perfect luau pizza. There are limits, even for me! Just be careful you don't load up on toppings that mean fat: pepperoni, vegetables drenched in oil, or a half pound of shredded full-fat cheese. If you are really artistic, create little faces with the toppings.

And for the bottoms, feel free to stray in other directions: frozen pizza dough is an obvious choice; but there's also pita bread, flour or corn tortillas, English muffins we all know about, or even matzoh for a very crispy no-bake crust. See—pizza can take on an ethnic personality that goes beyond Italian.

Oven-Fresh Monogrammed Breadsticks

Prep: 10 minutes
Bake: 375° for 10 to 12 minutes

I love these breadsticks. I shape them into initials—my own, friends who are having birthdays or anniversaries, and even names of states. And I serve them with a selection of mustards, just like you do with pretzels.

Nonstick vegetable oil cooking spray
All-purpose flour, for rolling
12 pieces (1 ounce each) frozen bread roll dough or bread dough, thawed
Salt-free spicy seasoning (optional)
Salt-free garlic herb seasoning (optional)
Poppy seeds (optional)
Sesame seeds (optional)

1 Preheat oven to 375°. Coat 2 nonstick baking sheets with cooking spray. With floured hands, roll each piece of dough back and forth between hands into long thin breadstick shape (about ½ inch thick and 12 inches long).

2 Sprinkle your choice of seasoning and/or seeds onto work surface. Roll breadstick dough over seasoning/seeds. Leave as sticks, or shape into letters for your initials, abbreviations of states, or whatever. Arrange breadsticks, ¾ inch apart, on prepared baking sheets.

3 Bake 10 to 12 minutes, until golden brown and crispy. Cool on wire rack.

NUTRIENT VALUE PER SERVING
(WITHOUT SEASONINGS
AND/OR SEEDS)
71 calories   3 g protein
1 g fat (15% fat)   13 g carbohydrate
139 mg sodium   0 mg cholesterol

A Potpourri of Mustards

Did you know that Grey Poupon, that tangy Dijon mustard eaten in the back seat of Rolls Royces, was created in 1777 by two men, Grey and Poupon? Grey was the important one—he had the recipe. Poupon only had the money. French's mustard was originated by George French in 1904—the same year the hot dog made its debut at the St. Louis World's Fair.

American mustard is the familiar yellow mustard, mild and slightly sweet. Perfect for our favorite dog. **Dijon mustard** has white wine in it and has a sharper flavor than the American version. **German mustards** can range from very hot to mild and sweet. Then, there are **flavored mustards:** usually a Dijon-style mustard, with **black pepper, horseradish, tarragon, honey, cranberry,** or even **mayonnaise** mixed in. And as if that weren't enough choices, there are also coarse-grained varieties.

Want to Know More About Mustards?
Visit the Mustard Museum in Mount Horeb, Wisconsin—more than 1,000 different mustards, with all 50 states represented.

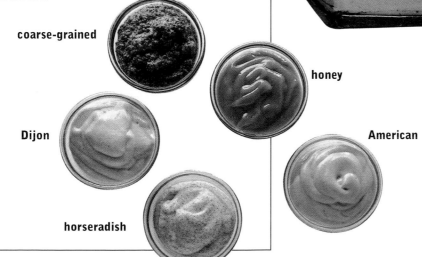

coarse-grained

Dijon

honey

American

horseradish

$\mathcal{C}$arnival Confetti Potatoes

Prep: 15 minutes
Bake: 400° for 30 minutes
Cook: 15 minutes

I remember when the caviar version of this was invented: little potatoes, scooped out and filled with sour cream and topped with caviar. I could easily have that for dinner—about fifteen of them. My recipe is much more sensible. Bring out a platter of these and it's an instant party. But you already know the problem—portion control. If you're not careful, one person will eat the entire tray when your back is turned, that's how good these are! Make sure you get really tiny red potatoes for this recipe—practically bite-size.

NUTRIENT VALUE PER SERVING
61 calories   3 g protein
trace of fat (2% fat)   12 g carbohydrate
138 mg sodium   1 mg cholesterol

1 pound baby rose potatoes *or* very small
 red potatoes
Nonstick olive oil cooking spray

RATATOUILLE
1 cup very small diced eggplant
Salt, for sprinkling
½ cup *each* very small diced zucchini *and*
 yellow squash *and* red *and* green bell
 peppers
Pinch of salt

CREAM CHEESE SPREAD
4 ounces fat-free cream cheese
1 to 2 teaspoons finely minced garlic
3 tablespoons finely minced fresh basil *or*
 1 teaspoon dried

1 Preheat oven to 400°. Wash potatoes.
 Cut in half. Coat nonstick baking sheet
 with cooking spray. Place potatoes, cut
 side down, on baking sheet.

2 Bake 30 minutes or until tender.

3 Ratatouille: Sprinkle eggplant lightly
 with salt and place in colander over sink
 to drain for 30 minutes. Pat excess
 moisture from eggplant pieces with
 paper towels.

4 Coat nonstick skillet with cooking
 spray. Heat over medium-high heat.

Cook zucchini and yellow squash 2 to 3
minutes, stirring frequently. Add both
bell peppers. Cook over medium-high
heat 4 minutes more, stirring
constantly. Add eggplant. Lower heat.
Cook 5 minutes more, stirring
occasionally. Add salt. Spoon into bowl.

5 Cream Cheese Spread: In small bowl
 mix cream cheese with garlic and basil.
 Cut small slice from rounded side of
 potatoes so that they sit flat with cut side
 up. Spread a little cream cheese mixture
 on each potato. Dip cream cheese top of
 each potato into ratatouille. Arrange on
 platter. Serve.

Other Uses

The ratatouille is an excellent topping for my mini pizzas
(page 28) or just spoon it on a reduced-fat cracker for a
snack. And a little dab of the cream cheese spread is
heaven on a baked potato.

atch, New Mexico, Fresh Tomato Salsa

MAKES 2 CUPS

Prep: 10 minutes
Stand: 30 minutes

One Labor Day weekend I tried to fly into Hatch, New Mexico. Forget it! The airport was closed. On that weekend every year, the runways and hangar are converted into a huge chile festival. (So I had to fly to El Paso, eighty miles away.) These chiles, New Mexico's biggest cash crop, became the inspiration for my salsa. My version is easy—it takes about 10 minutes to toss together, and that's moving slow. And depending on which of the chiles you use, you may be moving fast.

1½ cups diced fresh tomatoes
1 tablespoon diced seeded fresh *or* canned jalapeño pepper (see other chile choices, opposite)
3 tablespoons finely diced onion
2 tablespoons finely chopped fresh cilantro
1 tablespoon balsamic vinegar *or* fresh lime juice
1 clove garlic, minced
¼ teaspoon salt

In medium bowl combine all ingredients. Let stand, covered, at room temperature for 30 minutes.

What Do I Do with My Salsa?

- For a hot fondue salsa, mix a little reduced-fat Monterey Jack or cheddar cheese with the salsa and heat it up in a microwave oven on medium or half power. Absolutely delicious with raw vegetables for dipping—carrots, blanched broccoli flowerets, string beans, or sugar-snap peas. Also good with baked low-fat chips or corn tortilla wedges you bake in the oven until crispy.
- Stir into nonfat sour cream for a baked-potato topping.
- Mix into a reduced-fat or nonfat salad dressing for extra zip.
- Whisk a little into soup just before serving for a blast of flavor.
- Combine with your favorite meatloaf mixture.

You get the idea. Now see why salsa is the ketchup of the nineties?

Not a Lot of Fat

Here's one of those nutrition oddities. Even though there's hardly any measurable fat in this salsa, the percentage of calories from fat is 9%. How can that be? The reason is that the numbers themselves are small. There are practically no calories, a mere 3. It's like when you have two potato chips and you've eaten one—you've eaten 50%. Even though the numbers are low, the percentage is high.

NUTRIENT VALUE PER
TABLESPOON
3 calories   0 g protein
trace of fat (9% fat)   1 g carbohydrate
18 mg sodium   0 mg cholesterol

How Hot Do You Like Your Salsa?

Pick one of these, chop it, and toss it into the salsa:

Mild—anaheim chile, long and narrow and green.

Hot—jalapeño chile, short and stubby and green.

Very hot—serrano chile, tiny, thin and curvy, and can be red or green.

Off the charts—habanero chile, 2 inches long, lantern shaped, and dark green to orange, and when fully ripe, a red color that screams a warning: fifty times hotter than the jalapeño (and not recommended for the faint of heart).

Can't Stand the Heat?

To tame a chile pepper, slice the pepper in half lengthwise, scrape out the seeds, and cut away the membranes—that's where all the tear-causing heat is. To play it safe, wear rubber gloves. And whatever you do, don't scratch your eyes or touch any other sensitive spot on your body until everything is well scrubbed—or you'll know why grizzly bears stay clear of pepper plants.

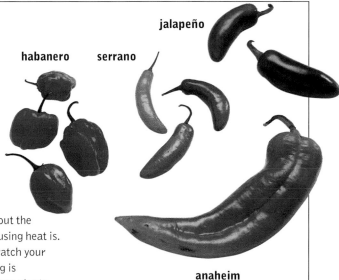

jalapeño

habanero   serrano

anaheim

Windy City Pesto and Ricotta Torta

MAKES 16 APPETIZER SERVINGS

Prep: 30 minutes
Bake: 350° for 45 to 60 minutes

I know what you're thinking: This is the most complicated recipe in the book. You're right! But if I can do it, so can you. Just save this recipe for special occasions. If you start a day ahead, and follow the directions slowly, step by step, inch by inch, half cup by half cup, I know you'll rise to the challenge. I gasped when I saw my first layered torta. It was in an Italian deli in Chicago—the torta's colors were the same as the Italian flag. *Mama mia!* But there was one problem: the fat content. I was immediately rushed to the hospital and put on antidepressants. But I rose to the challenge. After much tinkering in my kitchen, here it is: my very own reduced-fat version. It's *simpatico.*

NUTRIENT VALUE PER SERVING
54 calories   4 g protein
3 g fat (44% fat)   3 g carbohydrate
231 mg sodium   6 mg cholesterol

SUN-DRIED TOMATO PESTO
- ½ cup packed sun-dried tomatoes, dry pack
- 1 cup boiling water
- 1 tablespoon extra-virgin olive oil
- 2 teaspoons minced garlic
- ⅓ cup fat-free reduced-sodium chicken broth

CHEESE FILLING
- 1 container (8 ounces) low-fat ricotta cheese
- 4 ounces fat-free cream cheese
- 2 tablespoons grated Parmesan cheese
- ¼ cup liquid egg replacement
- ¼ teaspoon salt

BASIL PESTO
- 1 cup packed fresh basil leaves
- 2 teaspoons minced garlic
- ¼ cup chopped fresh parsley
- 2 tablespoons grated Parmesan cheese
- ⅓ cup fat-free reduced-sodium chicken broth
- ¼ teaspoon salt
- ⅛ teaspoon freshly ground black pepper

TO ASSEMBLE TORTA
- Nonstick vegetable oil cooking spray
- 2 tablespoons Italian-flavored dry bread crumbs
- Sprigs of fresh basil, for garnish (optional)

1 Tomato Pesto: In small bowl, soak sun-dried tomatoes in boiling water for 30 minutes or until softened. Drain, reserving ⅓ cup liquid.

2 In blender or food processor, combine tomatoes, reserved liquid, olive oil, garlic, and chicken broth. Process until smooth.

3 Cheese Filling: Iin blender or food processor, combine all cheeses, egg replacement, and salt. Process until smooth.

4 Basil Pesto: In blender or processor, combine basil, garlic, parsley, cheese, broth, salt, and pepper. Process until smooth.

5 Preheat oven to 350°. Coat 1-quart springform pan, tube pan, soufflé dish, or other straight-sided baking dish with cooking spray. Dust with Italian-flavored dry bread crumbs.

6 Divide cheese filling into 4 equal portions. Divide Sun-Dried Tomato Pesto in half. Spread one-quarter of cheese filling over bottom of pan. For next layer, spread half of Sun-Dried Tomato Pesto over cheese. Layer with another portion of cheese, followed by all of the Basil Pesto. Spread on another layer of cheese filling, then the remaining red pesto. Finally, cover the top with the remaining portion of cheese. (Layers should be white, red, white, green, white, red, and white.)

7 Bake 45 to 60 minutes, until top begins to brown and mixture begins to pull away from sides of pan. Cool in pan on wire rack. Chill several hours or overnight. Release springform. Unmold if center tube is present. (If in soufflé dish, serve directly from dish.) Garnish with basil, if desired. Serve sliced with fat-free crackers or French bread.

Bonus: Pasta Sauces

Use the pestos for these simple throw-together pastas. Toss Sun-Dried Tomato Pesto with 12 ounces of cooked, drained pasta. Or, combine tomato pesto with Basil Pesto, and toss with same amount of pasta. A sprinkle of pepper and Parmesan, and you'll be hearing Italian love songs.

Angel Eggs

Prep: 15 minutes
Stand: 20 minutes

These may look devilish, but they aren't—practically no fat and no cholesterol. It all vanishes with the egg yolks. Turn the page for my special *faux* guacamole filling.

6 large eggs
¾ cup It's Not Easy Being a Green Dip (page 40)
24 thin pimiento strips
Extra peas, for garnish (optional)

1 Using a small safety pin or egg piercer, pierce eggs in round end of shell. Place eggs in medium saucepan. Cover with cold water.

2 Bring to boil over medium-high heat. Remove pan from heat. Cover and let stand 20 minutes.

3 Plunge eggs immediately into cold water. Crack shells and peel. Cut eggs in half lengthwise. Discard yolks.

4 Place dip in pastry bag fitted with star tip. Or place in sealable plastic bag, seal, and snip off one corner of bag. Pipe dip into egg whites. Decorate each with 2 thin strips of pimiento and extra peas, if desired.

Other Fillings

- Hatch, New Mexico, Fresh Tomato Salsa (page 34)
- Tuna salad from Afternooner Tuna Sandwich (page 58)
- An American Quilt Chopped Salad (page 72)
- Ratatouille from Carnival Confetti Potatoes (page 32)

NUTRIENT VALUE PER SERVING
24 calories   3 g protein
trace of fat (8% fat)   3 g carbohydrate
73 mg sodium   0 mg cholesterol

It's Not Easy Being a Green Dip

MAKES 2 CUPS
Prep: 10 minutes
Stand: 2 hours

Many people just don't like the color green. In fact, we took a survey and discovered that the color people most disliked in food was green. So now we're going to change all that. We're advocates of making more food green—we mean green! You may think this dip is guacamole, but surprise!—an avocado has not even been in the same room with this. So forget the guacamole. This is a spicy garbanzo bean dip, made green with peas. Serve it in the same places you would guacamole, but just don't call it that.

1 can (15 ounces) garbanzo beans, drained and rinsed
1 cup frozen peas, thawed
¼ cup nonfat sour cream
4 green onions (green and white parts), chopped
2 cloves garlic, peeled
2 tablespoons *each* canned diced mild chilies *and* green hot-pepper sauce
1 to 2 tablespoons fresh lime juice
½ teaspoon ground cumin
¼ teaspoon salt

Place all ingredients in blender and puree until smooth. Let stand 2 hours to allow flavors to mellow.

NUTRIENT VALUE PER
TABLESPOON
23 calories   1 g protein
0 g fat (0% fat)   4 g carbohydrate
29 mg sodium   0 mg cholesterol

Santa Fe Tortilla Soup

MAKES 4 SERVINGS

Prep: 15 minutes
Cook: 20 minutes
Bake: 400° for 5 to 8 minutes

I love the way this soup looks—so festive, perfect for a party. And the colors remind me of Santa Fe where I've had this soup many times. When I make it at home, I like to arrange the garnishes—the tortilla strips, green onion, avocado, cilantro, and lime slices—in small pottery bowls and let my guests decorate away to their hearts' content. I've always thought there is a little of the decorator in all of us.

NUTRIENT VALUE PER SERVING
199 calories   21 g protein
5 g fat (21% fat)   20 g carbohydrate
983 mg sodium   44 mg cholesterol

2 cans (14½ ounces *each*) fat-free reduced-sodium chicken broth

1 cup diced onion

2 cloves garlic, minced

1 teaspoon *plus* 1 tablespoon chopped fresh cilantro *or* parsley

¾ teaspoon dried cumin

½ teaspoon salt

⅛ teaspoon pepper

8 ounces chicken tenders, diced small (see below)

2 corn tortillas

12 ounces plum tomatoes, peeled, seeded, and diced medium (page 18), *or* 1 can (14½ ounces) whole tomatoes, drained, seeded, and diced medium

1 tablespoon diced canned mild chilies

2 to 3 limes, juiced

2 tablespoons chopped green onion (green and white parts)

2 ounces shredded reduced-fat cheddar *or* Monterey Jack cheese

¼ avocado, seeded, peeled, and cubed (optional)

4 slices lime, for garnish

1 In medium saucepan bring chicken broth to boil. Add onion, garlic, 1 teaspoon cilantro, cumin, salt, and pepper. Simmer over medium heat 5 minutes.

2 Preheat oven or toaster oven to 400°.

3 Add chicken to simmering soup. Stir, cover, and remove from heat. Let stand 10 minutes.

4 Meanwhile, cut tortillas in half. Cut crosswise into ¼-inch wide strips. Place strips on baking sheet. Bake in oven until crisp, 5 to 8 minutes.

5 Stir tomatoes and chilies into chicken mixture. Place over low heat just to heat through. Add lime juice to taste. Remove from heat.

6 Ladle soup into 4 bowls. Top each with green onion, shredded cheese, cubes of avocado if using, and the 1 tablespoon chopped cilantro. Scatter tortilla strips over top. Garnish with lime slices.

Sacred Fat

I've sneaked in a little avocado—that high-fat culprit—and shredded cheese. But the operative word is *little,* plus I only use these as a garnish. And take a look at the fat—less than 30 percent.

Chicken Tenders?

No, this is not an Elvis Presley song. It's the small tender fillet or strip from the underside of the chicken breast—its shape reminds me of the map of Italy (a little boot). There's not a lot of waste with this, and you can easily toss leftovers into the freezer.

Newbury Street Clam Chowder

Prep: 15 minutes
Cook: 15 minutes

This New England classic really started in coastal villages in France several centuries ago. When the fishing fleet returned home, each man tossed part of his catch into a large pot to make a soup celebrating their safe return from the sea. (I get so excited returning safely home from the supermarket, I throw a party!) Eventually this tradition found its way to New England. Stroll along Boston's fashionable Newbury Street, and you'll find all kinds of versions being served in cafes.

Nonstick vegetable oil cooking spray
1 cup *each* finely chopped onion *and* finely diced celery
1 can (14½ ounces) fat-free reduced-sodium chicken broth
3 cups peeled, cubed potatoes
⅛ teaspoon *each* dried basil *and* thyme *and* marjoram
2 cans (6½ ounces *each*) chopped clams, drained, and juice reserved
½ cup evaporated skim milk
Paprika, for garnish
Snipped fresh chives, for garnish

1 Coat nonstick medium saucepan with cooking spray. Heat over medium-high heat. Add onion and celery. Cook, stirring constantly, until onion is softened, about 4 minutes. Add splash of chicken broth as needed to prevent onion sticking or overbrowning. Add potatoes and remaining chicken broth. Bring to boil. Cover, reduce heat, and simmer 10 minutes or until vegetables are tender. Remove from heat.

2 With slotted spoon, transfer half of cooked vegetable mixture to blender. Add herbs and ½ cup of reserved clam juice. Blend until smooth.

3 Return pureed mixture to remaining vegetable mixture in saucepan. Bring to simmer. Stir clams and milk into soup. Stir over low heat until clams are heated through. Do not boil.

4 Divide soup equally among 4 heated serving bowls. Garnish each with pinch of paprika and chives.

NUTRIENT VALUE PER SERVING
224 calories   18 g protein
1 g fat (5% fat)   35 g carbohydrate
490 mg sodium   34 mg cholesterol

Red or White

The original clam chowder was white—the basics were clams, salt pork, and milk. Then some Manhattan people said, "Let's change the ingredients and call it Manhattan Clam Chowder." Out came the milk, and in went tomatoes and water. New Englanders were horrified, as they are to this day.

Low-Fat Tricks

No heavy cream or butter in my version—just a little skim milk. To create a creamy thickness, without flour or cornstarch, I puree some of the vegetables, including the potato, and stir that back into the chowder. For practically no-fat sautéing, I cook the vegetables in a skillet coated with nonstick cooking spray, and then add a little chicken broth as needed to prevent sticking and overbrowning.

Uncanned Jersey City Tomato Soup

MAKES 4 SERVINGS

Prep: 15 minutes
Cook: 35 minutes

I'm from New Orleans, and I love the Creole tomato. But I grew up never knowing it had a brother, the New Jersey Beefsteak tomato. That big, beefy, juicy tomato smells and feels homegrown. And just because you don't live in New Jersey doesn't mean you can't have one. They travel—check out your produce section.

Basmati Rice

This is a long-grain aromatic rice from India and Pakistan now grown in the U.S.A. Its nutty taste makes it a nice switch from white rice. You'll find it in the rice section of your market.

NUTRIENT VALUE PER SERVING:
99 calories   3 g protein
1 g fat (6% fat)   22 g carbohydrate
560 mg sodium   0 mg cholesterol

Nonstick olive oil cooking spray
½ cup diced onion
1 can (14½ ounces) fat-free reduced-
sodium chicken broth
1 teaspoon dried basil
½ teaspoon paprika
¼ cup uncooked basmati rice
1 pound fresh tomatoes, peeled, seeded,
and chopped (page 18) *or* 1 can
(16 ounces) whole tomatoes, drained
and chopped
1¼ cups tomato juice
½ teaspoon sugar
Salt, to taste (optional)
4 sprigs fresh basil, for garnish (optional)

1 Coat large nonstick saucepan with cooking spray. Heat over medium-high heat. Add onion. Cook 1 minute, stirring constantly.

2 Add chicken broth, dried basil, and paprika. Simmer 2 minutes. Bring to boil. Add rice. Cover. Reduce heat. Simmer 20 minutes.

3 Add tomatoes, tomato juice, and sugar. Simmer 10 minutes.

4 Taste and add salt if needed. Ladle soup into heated serving bowls. Garnish each with sprig of basil.

You Say Tomato . . .

Fruit or Vegetable?
No matter what everybody says, a tomato is really a fruit. In 1893, for trade purposes, the government decided to call this fruit a vegetable. Just goes to show you, you can't trust the government with anything, can you?

How Healthy Is a Tomato?
One medium tomato supplies almost half of the vitamin C you need daily, as well as about 20 percent of the vitamin A, plus fiber and essential minerals.

Get the Best from Your Tomato
• Don't refrigerate a tomato—it ruins the flavor.
• To ripen, keep the tomato on the counter rather than on a sunny window sill, where it will "bake." To speed up the process, put the tomato in a brown paper bag with a ripe apple—the apple gives off a natural gas that helps the tomato ripen.

Which Tomato?
Red round tomatoes include the beefsteak and a whole host of other varieties. **Yellow round** are sweeter and less acidic than their red cousins. **Red or yellow plum tomatoes,** sometimes called **roma,** are a good bet for the winter months when most out-of-season tomatoes are tasteless. Their meaty pulp makes them ideal for sauces. **Red or yellow cherry tomatoes and pear tomatoes** are extra sweet and very pretty in salads, as a garnish, or quickly sautéed in a nonstick skillet with fresh herbs for an easy side dish. What I like is the explosion of flavor you get when you bite down on a whole one—just make sure to keep your mouth closed to avoid squirting family and friends. **Green tomatoes** are just an unripened tomato. (You remember the movie.) Instead of frying, coat slices with a little nonstick cooking spray, dip in cornmeal, spritz again with a little spray, and bake in a 350° oven until lightly golden.

beefsteak   plum   yellow

cherry

yellow pear

Campfire Vegetable-Bean-Pasta Soup

MAKES 6 SERVINGS

Prep: 10 minutes
Cook: 20 minutes

When I was little—I mean when I was young—my parents did the worst thing to me. They sent *me* to summer camp. It was horrifying! I like camp, but camping is not for me. (Or is it the other way around?) But believe it or not, one good thing did happen. I made a friend—the cook, Oscar. Who else? He shared with me this recipe for a hearty campfire soup, without the tent. Over the years I've added my own twist: couscous. Don't laugh. You probably thought it was a dance.

Nonstick olive oil cooking spray
1 cup chopped onion
2 cloves garlic, chopped
2 cans (14½ ounces *each*) fat-free reduced-sodium chicken broth
1 can (about 15 ounces) *each* garbanzo beans (chickpeas) *and* red kidney beans, drained and rinsed
2 teaspoons curry powder
¼ teaspoon salt
1½ cups water
1 cup sliced carrots
¾ cup small pasta shells
1 cup half-moon slices zucchini
¼ cup couscous
Half of 10-ounce package frozen chopped spinach, thawed, and squeezed dry *or* 6 ounces fresh spinach, stemmed, washed, dried, and shredded
1 to 2 tablespoons fresh lemon juice

All the Protein You Need, Without the Meat.

In this soup I combine complementary proteins, like beans and pasta and couscous. What that means is this: Each contains some of the essential amino acids found in protein, and taken all together, you get all of the amino acids. And what's important is that these are nonanimal sources, so you get no cholesterol or extra fat. Not a bad deal!

NUTRIENT VALUE PER SERVING
381 calories   20 g protein
3 g fat (8% fat)   71 g carbohydrate
1,202 mg sodium   0 mg cholesterol

1 Coat large Dutch oven with cooking spray. Heat over medium-high heat. Add onion and garlic. Cook, stirring, 2 minutes. Add splash of chicken broth as needed to prevent onion from sticking or browning.

2 To Dutch oven add beans, curry powder, salt, remaining chicken broth, and water. Bring to boil. Add carrots. Lower heat and simmer 5 minutes. Add pasta. Simmer 5 more minutes.

3 Add zucchini, couscous, and spinach. Simmer, stirring occasionally, 5 more minutes or until couscous and pasta are tender.

4 Stir in lemon juice. Adjust salt to taste.

Couscous

These are tiny granules of semolina. And so what's semolina? It's from durum wheat and is the same stuff used for making pasta. The type of couscous you usually find in the supermarket is quick-cooking, which means it's ready in ten minutes or less. I like to use it instead of rice for a change, and in soup it's perfect for thickening and adding texure.

Chicken Noodle Keep-Away-the-Flu Soup

MAKES 4 SERVINGS
Prep: 10 minutes
Cook: 25 minutes

I like my chicken soup simple and honest—like me. I know I'm probably going to get mail, but this is one of those cases where simplest is best: no rice, no matzoh balls, no culinary *chachkas*—just chicken, broth, a few vegetables, and a handful of noodles. At the first sign of a sniffle (God Bless You!), make a pot of this—it takes practically no time to fix.

2 cans (14½ ounces *each*) fat-free reduced-sodium chicken broth
½ cup water
8 ounces chicken tenders (see page 43)
½ cup chopped onion
1 cup *each* sliced carrots *and* celery *and* zucchini *and* mushrooms
⅔ cup broken egg noodles
¼ cup chopped fresh parsley
Salt and freshly ground black pepper, to taste

1 In medium saucepan bring chicken broth and water to boil over medium heat. Add chicken. Stir, cover, and remove from heat. Let stand 10 minutes. Chicken will cook perfectly. Lift chicken from broth with slotted spoon and set aside to cool.

2 Return broth mixture in saucepan to boil. Add onion, carrots, and celery. Cook 10 minutes or until vegetables are tender. Add zucchini, mushrooms, and noodles. Cook 5 minutes more.

3 Shred chicken. Add to saucepan. Add a little more water if desired if soup is too thick for your taste. Heat through. Stir in parsley. Season the soup to taste with salt and pepper.

NUTRIENT VALUE PER SERVING
147 calories   15 g protein
4 g fat (23% fat)   13 g carbohydrate
627 mg sodium   38 mg cholesterol

Las Vegas Lucky Seven Vegetable Soup

MAKES 4 SERVINGS

Prep: 15 minutes
Cook: 20 minutes

There are actually only six vegetables in this soup, but I count the parsley. No matter what the number, this soup rates high on the nutrient score card—lucky for you. Plus, when you taste this, you'll think it's loaded with heavy cream, but it isn't. The pureed potatoes, along with all the other vegetables, will fool you every time. This makes an elegant first course or, with a green salad and some crusty bread, a light supper or lunch.

1½ cans (14½ ounces *each*) fat-free reduced-sodium chicken broth
1½ cups diced peeled potato
1 cup chopped leeks *or* onion *and* sliced carrots *and* sliced zucchini *and* diced peeled butternut squash *or* other winter squash
¼ cup frozen peas, thawed
2 tablespoons chopped flat-leaf parsley (optional)
Salt and freshly ground black pepper, to taste
Peas and parsley sprigs, for garnish (optional)

1 In medium saucepan bring chicken broth to boil over medium heat. Add all vegetables except peas. Cook, uncovered, 10 minutes. Add peas and parsley if using. Cook 5 minutes or until vegetables are very tender. Let cool slightly.

2 In two or three batches, remove vegetables with slotted spoon to blender or food processor, with a little liquid. Puree. Return to saucepan. Gently reheat. Season with salt and pepper. Garnish each serving with peas and parsley sprigs, if desired.

A Finishing Flourish

To be real naughty, place 1 teaspoon light butter (Sacred Fat) on top of each serving and gently swirl in, or do the same with a dollop of nonfat sour cream. For a lighter garnish, float 1 or 2 fresh chives in each bowl, or tumble in a few peas. Want a splash of color? Puree jarred roasted red peppers and drizzle a little of the puree over the top.

NUTRIENT VALUE PER SERVING
106 calories   3 g protein
1 g fat (3% fat)   23 g carbohydrate
513 mg sodium   0 mg cholesterol

$\mathcal{L}$one Star "Where's the Beef?" Chili

Prep: 15 minutes
Cook: 40 minutes

Good food is worth fighting over. Take chili, for example. Texans claim they invented it, while Mexicans politely disagree. Talk to someone from Cincinnati and they'll tell you, forget everybody else— it all started in the Queen City. My version here is vegetarian, with beans. Don't tell a Texan this—they'll challenge you to a shoot-out if a bean even walks in the same neighborhood as their chili. No beans allowed! But serve me a bowl of this without telling me what's in it, and I would swear it's got the beef.

NUTRIENT VALUE PER SERVING
207 calories   11 g protein
1 g fat (4% fat)   37 g carbohydrate
637 mg sodium   0 mg cholesterol

Nonstick olive oil cooking spray

2 cloves garlic, minced

½ cup *each* chopped onion *and* chopped green *and* red bell peppers

1 cup vegetable broth *or* fat-free reduced-sodium chicken broth

1 cup *each* sliced zucchini *and* yellow squash

1 can (15 ounces) ready-cut tomatoes

1 can (8 ounces) tomato sauce

1 can (15 ounces) *each* pinto beans *and* kidney beans, drained and rinsed

1 can (12 ounces) dark beer

1 teaspoon ground cumin

½ teaspoon *each* chili powder *and* paprika *and* dried oregano

¼ teaspoon *each* cayenne *and* freshly ground black pepper, or to taste

2 tablespoons balsamic vinegar

½ teaspoon salt

¼ cup chopped fresh cilantro

Fat-free flour tortillas (optional)

1 Coat heavy saucepan or Dutch oven with cooking spray. Heat over medium heat. Add garlic and onion. Cook, stirring, 3 minutes, until slightly softened. Add green and red bell peppers. Cook 2 minutes, adding splashes of broth as needed to prevent sticking

2 Add zucchini, yellow squash, and remaining broth. Cook 2 minutes. Add tomatoes, tomato sauce, beans, and beer. Turn heat to medium-high. Add cumin, chili powder, paprika, oregano, cayenne, and black pepper. Reduce heat. Simmer, uncovered, 30 minutes.

3 Stir in vinegar, salt, and cilantro. Remove from heat. Serve with tortillas, warmed according to the package directions, if desired.

Pinto Beans

Pinto is the Spanish word for "painted." You know what a pinto pony looks like—someone spilled paint on it. Well, the bean has the same look: reddish-brown streaks over a background of pale pink. Very colorful. This is the bean that is usually used for refried beans. If you can't find canned pinto beans, substitute pink beans or black beans, or just double the amount of red kidney beans.

Secret Ingredient

Texans would approve of this: a bottle of dark beer makes this chili taste "meaty." And as I've said before, don't worry, the Woman's Christian Temperance Union won't show up at your front door—the alcohol cooks off. Experiment with different beers: beer with a chile pepper added, bitter ale, natural spring water amber beer, Long Island dark beer, cranberry beer, wild rice beer, and on and on.

Once-in-a-Blue-Moon Cheeseburger

MAKES 6 SERVINGS

Prep: 15 minutes
Cook: 8 minutes

I was a vegetarian for about nine years. And then one morning I woke up screaming, "Prime rib! Prime rib!" And now I love meat, but only once in a blue moon. This is my very special hamburger, filled with a Sacred Fat—blue cheese. Yes, blue cheese. I love it! That's why I'll treat myself to one of these, even though it comes in at more than 30% calories from fat. These burgers are smaller than the half-pounders you may be used to, but the flavor is so intense you won't miss the extra meat. But promise one thing—you'll eat only one of these at one meal. In fact, these are filling enough you could split one with a friend.

NUTRIENT VALUE PER SERVING
362 calories   24 g protein
16 g fat (41% fat)   30 g carbohydrate
537 mg sodium   61 mg cholesterol

1 pound extra-lean ground beef
2 slices whole-wheat bread, finely crumbed
¼ cup finely chopped green onion (green and white parts)
¼ teaspoon freshly ground black pepper
Pinch of salt
2 ounces blue cheese, crumbled
Nonstick olive oil cooking spray
6 hamburger buns, warmed or toasted
Butter lettuce *or* Boston lettuce leaves
6 slices tomato

1 In medium bowl combine ground beef, bread crumbs, green onion, pepper, and salt. Shape into 12 equal patties. Lay patties out in pairs on wax paper. Divide cheese equally among 6 of the patties, covering surface. Press remaining patties on top and seal edges with fingers. No cheese should be peeking through.

2 Coat large skillet with cooking spray. Heat over medium-high heat. Add burgers. Cook 3 to 4 minutes on one side. Turn over. Cook 3 minutes longer or until cooked through.

3 Serve on buns with lettuce leaves and tomato slices.

Burgers Everywhere

Seventy-five per cent of all beef eaten in this country is in the form of hamburgers, which translates into about 14 million a day—that's a lot of grease.

Other Fillings

If blue cheese is not your favorite, then substitute reduced-fat cheddar or provolone. When I've been really good, I'll treat myself to buffalo mozzarella—it's made from buffalo milk, no kidding. If you don't want to overload the burger with cheese, try this: Sauté a chopped onion or shallot in a nonstick skillet coated with cooking spray. Toss in a handful of chopped mushrooms and cook until softened. Season with salt and pepper. Then add to the meat mixture.

$\mathcal{A}$fternooner Tuna Sandwich

Prep: 30 minutes

Like many of you, I went to Catholic school. And boy, did we have tuna sandwiches—it seemed like every day was Friday. The best were the ones my mother Shirley made. She is the Princess of Tuna Fish Salad (as well as the Queen of Potato Salad). Her preparation was almost spiritual. When she opened the can, I loved to peek inside: that little spiral design reminded me of the Ziegfeld Follies girls, doing one of their fabulous dance routines. She'd patiently and very slowly drain the oil from the can—none of this squishing the top with a fork. I could go on for pages about this ritual, but I know you're all getting hungry.

NUTRIENT VALUE PER SERVING
258 calories   20 g protein
3 g fat (12% fat)   37 g carbohydrate
799 mg sodium   24 mg cholesterol

1 14-inch Middle Eastern bread round (Lahvash, shepherd's bread, or Syrian bread)

2 cans (6 ounces *each*) water-packed white Albacore tuna, drained and flaked

⅓ cup chopped green onion (green and white parts)

¼ cup *each* finely chopped fresh parsley *and* chopped celery

3 tablespoons sweet pickle relish

½ teaspoon salt

Freshly ground black pepper, to taste

½ cup reduced-fat mayonnaise

3 fresh medium tomatoes, thinly sliced

1 European-style cucumber, peeled and thinly sliced lengthwise

Leafy green lettuce leaves, washed, dried, and chilled

1 Run bread under hot water just until moistened but not soggy. Wrap in clean damp towel. Set aside.

2 In medium bowl combine tuna, green onion, parsley, celery, relish, salt, pepper, and mayonnaise.

3 Spread mixture evenly over bread. Cover with tomato slices, then cucumber slices. Arrange lettuce leaves in single layer over all.

4 Roll bread up tightly to enclose filling. Wrap in plastic. Chill until ready to serve. (Can be made an hour or two ahead.)

5 Just before serving, remove wrap and slice bread in diagonal slices. Serve with a knife and fork.

European Cucumber

Often called English cucumbers or, are you ready, burpless. They're seedless, and it's the seeds that cause those sounds. These cukes are easily spotted in the market since they're long and skinny, and are frequently shrink-wrapped.

Other Breads

I learned about breads at an early age. My father took me around to the different bakeries in New Orleans, and that was the beginning. If you can't find the Lahvash for this sandwich, by all means use rye, whole wheat, dark, or whatever else strikes your fancy.

Mayonnaise

This is one of those instances where nonfat mayonnaise just won't do. It has to be reduced-fat to get that special, rich taste.

A Tuna Called Wanda

MAKES 4 SERVINGS

Prep: 15 minutes
Marinate: 30 minutes to 1 hour
Broil: 8 to 10 minutes

This is tunafish salad from heaven, or maybe actually from the magical kingdom beneath the sea, where Wanda lives. I was walking past a fish case in a supermarket, and there it was—an ahi tuna, looking so beautiful. And I thought, tuna sandwich! That was the inspiration for this sandwich. As a treat, here's a special flavor trick: mix the reduced-fat mayonnaise with a little chutney or mustard. And for a nice finish, serve with a fresh tangerine.

LIME VINAIGRETTE
¼ cup fresh lime juice
1 tablespoon *plus* 1 teaspoon honey
⅛ teaspoon ground ginger
Pinch of cayenne
1 tablespoon olive oil

1 pound fresh tuna (about 1 inch thick)
Nonstick olive oil cooking spray
4 slices French or sourdough bread
¼ cup reduced-fat mayonnaise
2 tablespoons Major Grey chutney, pieces chopped
8 small romaine lettuce leaves, washed, dried, and chilled
2 tablespoons *each* finely diced celery *and* red onion *and* green onion (green and white parts)
8 cherry tomatoes, halved

1 Vinaigrette: In small jar with tight-fitting lid combine all ingredients for vinaigrette. Cover tightly. Shake.

2 Combine tuna and 2 tablespoons vinaigrette in sealable plastic bag. Seal. Refrigerate to marinate 30 minutes to 1 hour, turning bag occasionally.

3 Preheat broiler. Coat shallow baking pan with cooking spray. Broil tuna, about 1 inch from heat source, 4 to 5 minutes per side or until just opaque in center.

4 Toast bread. In small bowl combine mayonnaise and chutney. Spread over toast. Cover with lettuce leaves. Break tuna into bite-size chunks. Arrange tuna over lettuce. Top with diced celery and onion. Garnish with tomatoes. Drizzle with remaining vinaigrette. Serve open-faced with knife and fork.

NUTRIENT VALUE PER SERVING
360 calories   29 g protein
11 g fat (28% fat)   36 g carbohydrate
424 mg sodium   42 mg cholesterol

Philadelphia Cheese Steak Sandwich

Prep: 10 minutes
Cook: 2 to 3 minutes
Broil: 1 minute

And you thought the Liberty Bell made Philadelphia famous? Wrong. It was Geno's, where Presidents and movie stars go for the best Philadelphia cheese steak sandwich, at 1219 South 9th — ooops, how did that slip out? Now you know where to go. But be prepared to wait in line. I remember my first sandwich there. I took a bite, and my lips trembled — it was pure pleasure, but I knew I had just committed a grave sin. I screamed for forgiveness. Twenty times up and down the Rocky steps was just barely enough penance. But rest easy — my version here is much less sinful, and you don't have to wait in line.

NUTRIENT VALUE PER SERVING
583 calories   41 g protein
15 g fat (21% fat)   78 g carbohydrate
950 mg sodium   54 mg cholesterol

Nonstick butter-flavored cooking spray
1 cup thinly sliced onion rings
½ cup *each* thinly sliced red *and* green bell peppers
12 ounces Swanky Flanky Steak (page 112), very thinly sliced
4 French bread *or* hoagie-style rolls, cut in half lengthwise
4 ounces reduced-fat cheddar *or* Muenster cheese, thinly sliced

1 Coat nonstick medium skillet with cooking spray. Heat over medium-high heat. Add onion and bell peppers. Cook, stirring constantly, 2 to 3 minutes, adding a little water from time to time to prevent sticking and overbrowning.

2 Preheat broiler. Divide sliced flank steak over opened rolls. Cover with onion mixture. Top with cheese.

3 Broil, close to heat source, 1 minute or until cheese is melted and bubbly.

How Can This Be Low-Fat?

Well, in my version of the classic sandwich, I add lots of bell pepper and onion, and the cheese is reduced-fat. Plus, I start out with one of the leanest cuts of beef, the flank steak. And for extra flavor, I marinate it. Want to cut the calories in half? Share the sandwich with a special friend.

Topless Chicken Sandwich

MAKES 4 SERVINGS

Prep: 10 minutes
Cook: 6 minutes
Broil: 4 minutes

I had just stopped at the drive-through window at Wendy's to pick up a broiled chicken sandwich. (Now you know: I'm not an android. I am human, and yes I do stop occasionally at drive-through windows. Why not—they're exciting! I get to sing my order through the microphone. Don't tell me you never did.) So, I was driving down Melrose Place, with this culinary passenger in the front seat with me. Whoosh came a gust of wind through the open windows, and off flew the top of the sandwich—smack, right against the windshield. What a good idea, I thought—I'll do a topless, low-fat version for my cookbook, right after I clean my windshield.

Nonstick butter-flavored cooking spray
1 cup thinly sliced red onion
1 clove garlic, minced
2 cups sliced mushrooms
8 ounces chicken tenders (page 43)
Fresh lemon juice, to taste
Paprika *and* dried basil *and* lemon-pepper seasoning, to taste
2 French bread *or* hoagie-style rolls, cut in half lengthwise
Dijon-style mustard with horseradish (optional)
Salt and freshly ground black pepper, to taste
⅓ cup *each* shredded reduced-fat sharp cheddar cheese *and* reduced-fat Monterey Jack cheese

1 Coat nonstick skillet with cooking spray. Heat over medium-high heat. Add onion, garlic, and mushrooms. Cook, stirring, until onion is golden and mushrooms are browned, about 6 minutes.

2 Preheat broiler. Cover broiler pan with aluminum foil. Coat foil with cooking spray. Arrange chicken tenders in single layer on broiler pan. Sprinkle with lemon juice, paprika, basil, and lemon-pepper seasoning.

3 Broil, 1 to 2 inches from heat source, for 2 minutes. Turn chicken over. Sprinkle with lemon juice, then the seasonings as before. Broil 1 minute more or until no longer pink in center.

4 Transfer chicken to cutting board. Slice diagonally across grain into small pieces.

NUTRIENT VALUE PER SERVING
353 calories 25 g protein
9 g fat (22% fat) 44 g carbohydrate
754 mg sodium 48 mg cholesterol

5 Broil opened rolls, cut side up, until lightly toasted. Spread with mustard, if using. Spoon onion and mushroom mixture onto both sides of rolls, dividing equally. Sprinkle with a little salt and pepper.

6 Divide chicken over onions and mushrooms. Top with cheeses.

7 Broil sandwiches, 1 to 2 inches from heat source, for 1 minute or until cheese has just melted. Serve open-faced, with knives and forks.

Popped-Corn Muffins with Jalapeño

MAKES 12 MUFFINS

Prep: 15 minutes
Cook: 4 minutes
Bake: 400° for 15 minutes

This is one of my favorites. Just talking about these muffins gets me salivating. But watch out—you can down a bunch of these in just a few minutes, and you don't want to do that. Portion control! I love serving a basket of these with my Uncanned Jersey City Tomato Soup (page 46), for a touch of the Southwest—corn and jalapeño pepper.

NUTRIENT VALUE PER MUFFIN
168 calories   10 g protein
3 g fat (15% fat)   25 g carbohydrate
222 mg sodium   27 mg cholesterol

Nonstick vegetable oil cooking spray

½ cup frozen whole-kernel corn, thawed, *or* canned, drained

⅓ cup chopped onion

¼ cup canned diced mild chilies

1 cup yellow cornmeal

1 cup all-purpose flour

¼ cup sugar

1 tablespoon baking powder

¼ teaspoon salt

2 large egg whites

1 cup low-fat buttermilk

¼ cup unsweetened applesauce

2 tablespoons vegetable oil

36 cubes (¼ inch each) fat-free jalapeño-flavored Monterey Jack cheese (about 9 ounces)

1 Preheat oven to 400°. Coat standard-size 12-cup muffin pan with cooking spray. Set aside.

2 Coat medium nonstick skillet lightly with cooking spray. Heat over medium-high heat. Add corn, onion, and chilies. Cook until onion starts to brown and corn makes popping noises, 3 to 4 minutes. Set aside to cool.

3 In large bowl combine cornmeal, flour, sugar, baking powder, and salt. Add corn mixture. Toss to coat thoroughly with flour mixture. Make a well in center.

4 In medium bowl beat egg whites with electric beater or whisk until soft peaks form. In small bowl combine buttermilk, applesauce, and oil. Fold buttermilk mixture gently into egg whites until just combined.

5 Spoon egg white mixture into well in dry ingredients. Gently fold in with spatula until flour mixture is just moistened. Batter will be lumpy. Do not overmix.

6 Spoon batter into prepared muffin-pan cups, dividing equally. Push 3 cheese cubes halfway into top of each muffin.

7 Bake 15 minutes or until cheese cubes are tinged with brown and wooden pick inserted in centers of muffins comes out clean. Cool muffins in pan on wire rack 5 minutes. Then turn muffins out onto rack to cool completely.

Low-Fat Tricks

I use lots of low-fat ingredients here. First, rather than whole eggs, I use just the whites—no fat. Then there's buttermilk, which gives a rich taste that seems like fat, but there's none. And the secret ingredient—applesauce that adds a touch of sweetness and creates the illusion of fat. Fooled you again! And peeking out of the top of each muffin are tiny cubes of fat-free jalapeño cheese.

My Flavor Secret

You already know about popped corn (hold the butter, please!), but these are popped fresh (not dried) corn kernels. I heat up a nonstick skillet, toss in the corn kernels, and cook them just until they brown a little and begin to pop. They add a great toasty flavor to the muffins.

Circleville Pumpkin-Ginger Muffins

MAKES 12 MUFFINS

Prep: 10 minutes
Bake: 400° for 20 minutes

I had never heard of a pumpkin muffin until I first met one in Circleville, Ohio, at the annual pumpkin festival. And then I felt like Cinderella with a thousand coaches—all those pumpkins. These muffins are great by themselves as a pick-me-up in the afternoon with a cup of herbal tea—but remember, have just one! Or serve with my Las Vegas Lucky Seven Vegetable Soup (page 52) or Sunshine Stuffed Pork Chops (page 118).

Nonstick vegetable oil cooking spray
1¾ cups all-purpose flour
¼ cup chopped crystallized ginger
⅓ cup (packed) light brown sugar
2 teaspoons baking powder
¼ teaspoon *each* baking soda *and* nutmeg *and* salt
¼ cup liquid egg replacement
1 cup canned solid-pack pumpkin puree
¾ cup low-fat buttermilk
2 tablespoons vegetable oil

1 Preheat oven to 400°. Coat standard-size 12-cup muffin pan with cooking spray. In large bowl combine flour, ginger, sugar, baking powder, baking soda, nutmeg, and salt. Make a well in center.

2 In medium bowl beat egg replacement until foamy. Stir in pumpkin, buttermilk, and vegetable oil. Pour into well in flour mixture. Stir just until moistened. Batter should be lumpy. Do not overbeat.

3 Spoon batter into prepared muffin-pan cups. Do not overhandle mixture.

4 Bake 20 minutes or until golden and wooden pick inserted in centers of muffins comes out clean. Cool muffins in pan on wire rack several minutes. Then turn muffins out onto rack to cool. Best served while still slightly warm.

NUTRIENT VALUE PER MUFFIN
135 calories   5 g protein
3 g fat (18% fat)   24 g carbohydrate
165 mg sodium   1 mg cholesterol

Crystallized Ginger

What makes my muffins special is a touch of a Sacred Sweet: crystallized ginger—pieces of fresh ginger cooked in a sugar syrup. You got it—sugar, and that's calories. But just a little for flavor is not going to hurt you. I love to use this ginger for roasting chicken or a lean loin of pork. With a small paring knife, I make tiny slits all over the meat. Then instead of sticking in slivers of garlic, I push little pieces of crystallized ginger into the slits. It's magic—when the meat roasts, the ginger melts right into the meat. The Chinese have been using ginger for centuries. They have great respect for its tranquilizing properties and other healing characteristics.

NOT JUST ANOTHER

HEAD OF LETTUCE

An American Quilt Chopped Salad

MAKES 4 SERVINGS

Prep: 30 minutes

My mother, Shirley, learned early on with my perfect brother Lenny and Yours Truly running around the house that whacking a knife on a cutting board is very therapeutic—much cheaper than a therapist and healthier than tranquilizers. Thanks, Mom, I got my love of chopping from you. One of my favorite restaurants serves this salad at the table in separate colorful ribbons of ingredients, and then it's all tossed together with much clanging of spoons. It reminds me of an American patchwork quilt: the green of the rolling wheat fields of the plains states; the yellow sunshine of Florida with all its citrus groves; and the red mesa of Arizona.

NUTRIENT VALUE PER SERVING
69 calories   2 g protein
2 g fat (25% fat)   12 g carbohydrate
217 mg sodium   0 mg cholesterol

DRESSING

- 1 teaspoon minced garlic
- 2 tablespoons finely diced red onion
- 2 tablespoons Dijon-style mustard
- ⅓ cup balsamic vinegar
- 2 tablespoons reduced-sodium soy sauce
- 1 tablespoon plus 1 teaspoon olive oil
- 1 teaspoon *each* arrowroot *and* honey
- ¼ teaspoon salt

- ½ cup *each* finely chopped cucumber (peeled or unpeeled) *and* celery *and* red onion *and* carrot *and* green beans
- ½ cup fresh corn kernels *or* frozen, thawed, *or* canned, drained
- ½ cup finely diced radicchio *or* red cabbage

Lettuce leaves *or* red cabbage leaves, for serving

1 Dressing: Place all dressing ingredients in blender. Blend until well mixed; there will still be little pieces of onion. Pour into small saucepan. Heat gently, stirring. Do not boil. Let cool. Then chill. You should have about ¾ cup dressing.

2 In serving bowl combine all chopped and diced vegetables. Chill. Just before serving, add ¼ cup dressing to vegetables in bowl. Toss to combine. Taste and add more dressing if you like. Arrange each portion of salad on a lettuce leaf or red cabbage leaf on a serving plate.

A Sour Note

Remember when there was just white vinegar and cider vinegar, and you used it for salad dressings? No more! Now there are all kinds, and it's a great way to add flavor to sauces, marinades, and many dishes, without adding fat. Check out the vinegar section in your supermarket. Here are just a few. Pictured from left to right:

Distilled white vinegar is very acidic and is best used for pickling.

Balsamic vinegar is a dark vinegar made from unfermented grapes and aged in wooden casks for a strong, mellow flavor. The best comes from Italy. Sprinkle a little on cut-up fresh fruit or berries for an easy dessert. Really!

Rice vinegar is sweet and not as sharp as other vinegars. Used in Asian cooking, it adds a mild flavor to any dish.

Herb vinegars are usually made from white wine vinegar and contain fresh herbs such as tarragon, basil, or dill. Delicious for flavoring poultry or vegetable dishes and salad dressings.

Wine vinegars can be used anywhere. **Red wine vinegar** is good in marinades and stands up well to strong flavors, such as assertive salad greens (escarole or spinach), while the **white** is much milder and works well with delicate greens (red leaf, Bibb) and in poultry and fish dishes.

Cider vinegar is made from fermented apple juice. Its mildly acidic, almost sweet flavor is delicious in potato salad and cole slaw.

An-Apple-a-Day Coleslaw

MAKES 4 SERVINGS

Prep: 15 minutes

First I thought of naming this recipe Apple Slaw, but that sounded like a slaughter on Tenth Avenue. You know, all those apples and cabbage slugging it out. I like my food peaceful. Mealtime should be relaxed and a time when we can share—better for the digestion. The apples make this coleslaw even better than a regular one, so the recipe name is about keeping the doctor away.

DRESSING

1 cup low-fat buttermilk
½ cup reduced-fat mayonnaise
2 tablespoons rice wine vinegar
1 tablespoon Dijon-style mustard
2 teaspoons sugar
¼ to ½ teaspoon salt

SLAW

2 green apples, such as Pippin or Granny Smith, peeled, cored, and cut up
1 tablespoon rice wine vinegar
1 cup shredded carrots
½ cup finely diced green onion (green and white parts)
2 cups *each* chopped green cabbage *and* red cabbage

1 Dressing: In large serving bowl whisk all dressing ingredients together.

2 Slaw: In medium bowl toss apple pieces in rice wine vinegar. Pour off excess vinegar. Add apples to dressing mixture in serving bowl. Toss to coat.

3 Add remaining slaw ingredients to serving bowl. Do not mix. Cover and chill until serving time. Just before serving, toss to coat all ingredients with dressing.

Creamy Dressing

Low-fat buttermilk and reduced-fat mayonnaise—those are the secret ingredients in my low-fat dressing, which is also delicious in potato salad or other vegetable salads. Once I drank a small cup of this, but that's between you and me.

NUTRIENT VALUE PER SERVING
158 calories 4 g protein
3 g fat (17% fat) 31 g carbohydrate
727 mg sodium 2 mg cholesterol

The Hidden Trees

Ask six different cooks how they shred cabbage and you'll get six different answers, and her or his way is the only way. Well, my way is best. First you cut the cabbage in half through the stem end, and then in quarters the same way. Now take a look. There are those hidden trees (or core), just like a Hallmark card—that's what my father called them. Cut those out—but wait, don't you dare throw them out. America is littered with graveyards full of these hidden trees—just like broccoli stalks. These trees are delicious. Arrange them in a starburst pattern (you can very lightly blanch them first) on a colorful platter with a little bowl of dip in the center—nothing fatty, please. Try my It's Not Easy Being a Green Dip (page 40) or Hatch, New Mexico, Fresh Tomato Salsa (page 34), or even nonfat sour cream. Now you can shred the rest of the cabbage any way you like.

The Secret Is in the Potatoes

My mother was ahead of her time when she first made potato salad. The neighbors all used russets, and peeled them. When Shirley said no to the russets, she broke all the rules. She instead boiled little red potatoes; plus, she didn't peel them. Imagine all those vitamins and minerals being tossed out in the garbage. So come picnic time, all the other salads in the neighborhood were naked, but not Shirley's; hers was dressed, with the skins still on!

My Mother's Potato Salad, a Little Remodeled

Prep: 15 minutes
Cook: 10 minutes

What could be more "hooray America!" than potato salad on the Fourth of July? My mother, Shirley, is the Queen of Potato Salad. This is her shining moment—her salad is beautiful. She drags out onto the counter that Marie Antoinette egg slicer. Whack! Hard-cooked eggs are instantly transformed into beautiful, flowerlike slices. These go on top of the salad, with a tiny radish or tomato rosette in the center of each. You don't want to eat this salad—you want to escort it to the prom! Sometimes, while the potatoes are still warm, she tosses them with vinegar for extra flavor. That's what I do in my recipe.

SALAD

- 4   cups cubed unpeeled red potatoes
- 1   can (14½ ounces) fat-free reduced-sodium chicken broth
- 2   tablespoons cider vinegar
- ¾   cup finely diced celery
- ½   cup finely diced green onion (green and white parts)
- 2   hard-cooked egg whites, coarsely chopped
- 1   tablespoon minced fresh parsley

DRESSING

- ½   cup reduced-fat mayonnaise
- 1   tablespoon *each* coarse-grained Dijon-style mustard *and* sweet pickle relish
- ¼   teaspoon salt
- ¼   teaspoon freshly ground black pepper
- ⅛   teaspoon celery seed

1 Salad: In medium saucepan combine potatoes and chicken broth. Bring to boil over medium heat. Cover and cook about 10 minutes or until tender. Drain and save cooking liquid to use for soup. In large bowl toss hot potatoes with vinegar.

2 Dressing: In second large bowl mix together dressing ingredients. Add cooled potatoes, together with remaining salad ingredients. Toss to combine. Chill before serving.

NUTRIENT VALUE PER SERVING
218 calories   6 g protein
2 g fat (9% fat)   44 g carbohydrate
887 mg sodium   0 mg cholesterol

In-the-Shade Tomato-Bread Salad

MAKES 4 SERVINGS

Prep: 20 minutes
Stand: 1 hour
Bake: 350° for 10 to 15 minutes

This is another one of those dishes that has been imported to this country, and is now everywhere. I first tasted it when I was an art student in Italy. When I saw this salad—some call it panzanella—it was like a beautiful painting. What made it so delicious was the olive oil. Not just a splash, but gallons of the most perfumy, rich olive oil you could ever imagine. (Sometimes I'd just dab a little behind my ears.) It was like the best lube job for an Italian racing car. My recipe is just as good, but with much less oil.

NUTRIENT VALUE PER SERVING
407 calories   12 g protein
9 g fat (20% fat)   70 g carbohydrate
911 mg sodium   0 mg cholesterol

2 pounds fresh tomatoes, peeled

Nonstick olive oil cooking spray

1 loaf (1 pound) Italian bread, cut into 1-inch cubes

2 teaspoons salt-free garlic-herb seasoning

2 cloves garlic, finely chopped

4 teaspoons extra-virgin olive oil

2 tablespoons tomato juice

1 tablespoon balsamic vinegar

¼ cup (packed) finely shredded fresh basil

¼ teaspoon salt

1 Cut tomatoes into bite-size pieces. Place in colander, sitting over bowl. Let sit 1 hour, tossing occasionally.

2 Preheat oven to 350°. Coat roasting pan with cooking spray. Add bread and herb seasoning. Toss to coat bread.

3 Bake, tossing frequently, 10 to 15 minutes or until bread is crisp and tinged golden brown. Set aside.

4 In large serving bowl combine garlic, olive oil, tomato juice, balsamic vinegar, basil and all juice collected in bowl from tomatoes. Add tomatoes and salt. Toss.

5 Arrange tomato mixture on serving platter. Scatter bread cubes over top. Just before serving, toss to combine.

The Right Fat

This salad has just 4 teaspoons of olive oil—that's just 1 teaspoon per person. And since the fat is coming from the olive oil, the majority of it is monounsaturated and polyunsaturated—it's good fat, which is thought to help lower cholesterol levels.

When and How to Serve

This salad is substantial enough for a light lunch or supper, with an assortment of salad greens on the side—so healthy. For an appetizer or first course, I divide the recipe into six servings, or even eight for just a taste. This smaller portion size is what I spoon into a lettuce cup for people when they stop by the house to visit. We always move toward the kitchen and gather around my butcher block table. When I serve this, the kitchen gets very quiet. Everyone is eating. Can you imagine—me, quiet?

Christmas Salad

Prep: 20 minutes
Cook: 5 minutes

I get all warm and tingly when I make this salad. It's the colors, red and green—it reminds me of Christmas. Here's a case again where the grams of fat are low, the calories are low, but the percent of fat is high. Remember, most of the fat is monounsaturated and polyunsaturated, which help keep cholesterol in check.

Tomato Peeling

My father had his own way of peeling a tomato—all in one move. With a small paring knife, he'd start at the stem end and peel off the skin in one continuous spiral, talking at the same time. It drove me crazy—I could never do it that way. Turn to page 18 for my easier method.

DRESSING
2 tablespoons red wine vinegar
2 tablespoons fresh lemon juice
¼ cup finely chopped fresh basil
1 clove garlic, minced
1 tablespoon *each* Dijon-style mustard *and* extra-virgin olive oil
¼ teaspoon salt
¼ teaspoon freshly ground black pepper

1 pound plum tomatoes, peeled and seeded
1 pound green beans, trimmed

1 Dressing: In small container with screw-top lid combine all dressing ingredients. Cover tightly and shake to mix. Set aside.

2 Cut tomatoes into bite-size pieces and place in medium bowl.

3 Cut beans into 2-inch lengths. Place in small saucepan with boiling water. Cook over medium heat until just barely tender, about 5 minutes. Drain. Cool immediately under cold tap water or in bowl of ice water. Drain. Blot dry with paper towels. Add beans to tomatoes.

4 Pour dressing over vegetables. Toss to combine. Transfer salad to serving bowl.

NUTRIENT VALUE PER SERVING
91 calories   3 g protein
4 g fat (37% fat)   14 g carbohydrate
239 mg sodium   0 mg cholesterol

Frenching the Beans

If you want to make this salad special for company, here's a little trick that will make all your guests think you trained at the Cordon Bleu—you know, that famous cooking school in France. Cut the green beans lengthwise into thin strips— it's called Frenching, and it's different than what kids used to do in the back seat of a Studebaker. It will take some time. You'll need to stand there for about 3 hours, with your bifocals on, cutting carefully away. But there is an easier way. Go to a kitchenware store or a hardware store. Look in the kitchen gadgets section for a swivel-bladed vegetable peeler, the kind with a Frencher on the end. It will be a little open box with two small cutters inside. All you do is push the beans lengthwise through the cutters, and there you have it. You don't believe me? Take a few green beans with you, a friend for a lookout, and try your own in-store demonstration.

The-Ladies-Who-Lunch Warm Spinach Salad

MAKES 4 SERVINGS

Prep: 15 minutes
Cook: 2 minutes

As a child, I never liked spinach. It always looked like it had been boiled to death—I wanted to have a funeral for it. It was so overcooked. Then when spinach salads became popular in the seventies, I would be invited to somebody's house, and there it would be—a gritty salad. When God created spinach he was very kind to it—he gave it lots of nutrients. But he forgot something—he didn't run it through the wash-and-dry cycle. He left that to us. Thanks!

NUTRIENT VALUE PER SERVING
188 calories   6 g protein
7 g fat (30% fat)   29 g carbohydrate
284 mg sodium   0 mg cholesterol

DRESSING

- 1 tablespoon plus 1 teaspoon olive oil
- 2 cloves garlic, crushed
- 1 cup finely chopped onion
- ½ cup balsamic vinegar
- 2 tablespoons chopped fresh mint
- 2 tablespoons fresh lemon juice
- 2 teaspoons country-style Dijon mustard
- 1 teaspoon sugar
- ½ teaspoon dried marjoram

SALAD

- 1 head butter lettuce *or* Boston lettuce
- 1 can (15 ounces) garbanzo beans (chickpeas), drained and rinsed
- 4 cups fresh spinach leaves, washed, dried, stacked, and shredded in ½-inch-wide strips
- 1 small head radicchio, leaves separated and torn

1 Dressing: In small saucepan heat oil over medium-high heat. Add garlic and onion. Cook, stirring, until onion is softened but not browned, 2 minutes. Stir in remaining dressing ingredients. Remove from heat. Keep warm.

2 Salad: Arrange some of the lettuce leaves on serving plates. Tear up remainder and place in serving bowl. Add garbanzo beans, spinach, and radicchio.

3 Just before serving, add warm dressing to salad in bowl. Toss to combine. Serve over lettuce leaves on plates.

Chiffonading

Before reading on, understand this has nothing to do with chiffon — neither the kind you wear or eat. I don't like large lettuce leaves. What I do, after snipping off the tough stems, is stack the leaves on top of each other like dollar bills — sometimes as many as a hundred — and then I cut them across in narrow shreds, like cutting fresh pasta. That's what's called cutting a chiffonade. The dressing for this salad is fabulous — little pieces of sautéed onion and fresh mint give it lots of texture.

Lots of Good Stuff

The spinach is a good source of iron and vitamins A and C, and the garbanzo beans (a.k.a. chickpeas) add even more iron as well as protein, calcium, and phosphorus.

Wash Those Leaves!

First, wash the leaves in a sink or basin of warm water. It's like a massage — the leaves relax and the deep-down dirt is loosened for easier removal. Repeat with several more changes of water, each time colder so the leaves begin to firm up. Then, dry the leaves in a salad spinner or blot with paper towels. There's nothing worse than drippy leaves diluting the salad dressing.

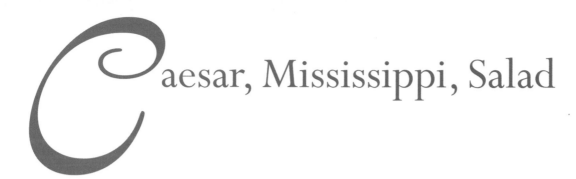

Caesar, Mississippi, Salad

MAKES 4 SERVINGS

Prep: 15 minutes
Chill: 1 hour

During my travels I once passed through Caesar, Mississippi, a town so small it's not on any map. And wouldn't you know it, I met a relative of the Caesar who invented the salad, right there in Mississippi. So forget all the stories you've heard about the salad coming from Mexico or Italy—they're just not true. Caesar's cousin helped me create this lower-fat version. One of the keys for a great Caesar salad is chilled greens—wash and dry them, wrap in paper toweling, and store in the refrigerator. Serve this salad on a cold plate with a cold fork.

1 head romaine lettuce
2 cloves garlic, peeled
¼ teaspoon *each* salt *and* freshly ground black pepper *and* sugar
1 teaspoon *each* Worcestershire sauce *and* Dijon-style mustard
2 tablespoons *each* fresh lemon juice *and* fat-free reduced-sodium chicken broth
1 tablespoon plus 1 teaspoon olive oil
2 cups baked bread cubes or croutons (see In-the-Shade Tomato-Bread Salad, page 78)
¼ cup grated Parmesan cheese

1 Wash, dry, and core romaine. Tear or shred crosswise into ½-inch wide strips or bite-size pieces. Wrap in paper towels. Chill for at least 1 hour.

2 In large wooden salad bowl sprinkle garlic cloves with salt. Using back of salad spoon, squash garlic and salt and mix into paste. Add pepper, sugar, Worcestershire sauce, and mustard. Whisk to mix. Whisk in lemon juice and chicken broth. Slowly whisk in olive oil until well blended and smooth.

3 Just before serving, add lettuce, bread cubes, and Parmesan cheese to salad bowl. Toss to thoroughly combine. Serve immediately.

NUTRIENT VALUE PER SERVING
145 calories   6 g protein
7 g fat (45% fat)   14 g carbohydrate
439 mg sodium   5 mg cholesterol

Croutons

Got to have great croutons. Caesar's cousin's croutons were tasty, but so greasy I squeezed out all the excess fat and fried up a batch of chicken in it. Here's the secret to my practically fat-free croutons — a very light coating of olive oil cooking spray. For really crisp croutons, lower the oven temperature to 325° and bake them until they're as crunchy as you like. Cut the bread into different shapes: triangles, diamonds, rounds, or even animal shapes. And try a variety of breads: Italian, French, even firm cornbread. To jazz up the flavor, before baking, sprinkle the bread with an herb or spice such as curry powder, chili powder, or basil.

Nutrition Lesson

Notice that the percentage of fat from calories is 45%. Whoooa! But look at the grams of fat — only 7, and not a lot of calories. This recipe uses Sacred Fat, in two forms, but in moderation — oil and cheese — and the taste is terrific. And the percentage of fat is much less than in the usual Caesar. So what does all this mean? Sometimes you need to treat yourself with a little fat, but not too much. And in this salad, most of the fat is polyunsaturated and monosaturated — good fats that may help lower cholesteol levels in your body, and in turn lower the risk of heart disease. Another option: mix up the dressing in a glass jar, and then pass it separately around the table with the undressed salad — let people drizzle their own dressing.

*T*wo Pasta Salads Are Better Than One

MAKES 6 SERVINGS

Prep: 15 minutes
Bake: 375° for 30 minutes
Cook: 20 minutes

Fifteen years ago, or maybe it was twenty, we began calling spaghetti "pasta." And then pasta found its way into salads. As I traveled around the country, I spotted pasta salads on restaurant menus. When I saw them in supermarket salad bars, I knew they were here to stay. It's what I call the "Noodling of America."

NUTRIENT VALUE PER SERVING
OF SALAD WITH
HERBAL VINAIGRETTE
199 calories   8 g protein
5 g fat (21% fat)   33 g carbohydrate
150 mg sodium   5 mg cholesterol

NUTRIENT VALUE PER SERVING
OF SALAD WITH
CREAMY DILL DRESSING
194 calories   9 g protein
3 g fat (15% fat)   34 g carbohydrate
148 mg sodium   5 mg cholesterol

4 cups diced unpeeled eggplant (1 medium)
2 cups fresh broccoli flowerets
½ pound penne pasta, cooked according to package directions and drained
2 cups cherry tomatoes, halved
½ cup chopped green onion (green and white parts)
2 ounces part-skim mozzarella cheese, cut in ¼-inch cubes

HERBAL VINAIGRETTE
2 tablespoons *each* chopped fresh cilantro *and* chopped fresh parsley *and* chopped fresh mint *and* chopped fresh basil
¼ cup red wine vinegar
1 tablespoon olive oil
¼ teaspoon salt

CREAMY DILL DRESSING
1 cup nonfat plain yogurt
½ cup reduced-fat mayonnaise
1 tablespoon Dijon-style mustard with horseradish
2 tablespoons chopped fresh dill *or* 2 teaspoons dried dill
1 tablespoon red wine vinegar
1 teaspoon sugar
¼ teaspoon salt

1 Preheat oven to 375°. Cover baking sheet with aluminum foil. Coat with cooking spray. Spread eggplant in single layer.

2 Bake eggplant 30 minutes, turning once or twice, or until tender.

Watch Out for the Dressing!

Most salads are pretty low in fat—it's what goes on them that can spell fat disaster. In my recipe I give you two low-fat choices: a vinaigrette—that's just another name for an oil-and-vinegar dressing—with lots of chopped fresh herbs but little oil; and a creamy dressing, made with nonfat yogurt and reduced-fat mayonnaise, which I think has better texture and flavor than the no-fat mayo. These dressings are delicious on any salad, from potato to green.

Shapely Salad

Penne, or quill-shaped pasta (that's what *penne* means in Italian), is what I use here. But **wagon wheels, fusilli, orechiette, rigatoni,** and **bow-ties** are other fun shapes. And if you can get the tricolor variety, or even all green or red, you can turn your salad into a technicolor noodle extravaganza.

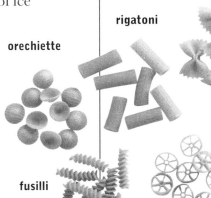

bow-ties

rigatoni

orechiette

fusilli

wagon wheels

penne

3 In a pot of boiling water cook broccoli briefly until barely tender. Drain. Chill immediately in bowl of ice water. Drain. Dry on paper towel.

4 In serving bowl combine baked eggplant, broccoli, penne, tomatoes, green onion, and cheese cubes.

5 Dressing: In blender or small food processor blend together ingredients for either Herbal Vinaigrette or Creamy Dill Dressing. Toss salad in dressing of choice.

AT HOME

ON THE RANGE

ecan Oven-Fried Chicken

MAKES 4 SERVINGS

Prep: 10 minutes
Marinate: 8 hours or overnight
Bake: 425° for 20 minutes, then
350° for 15 to 20 minutes

Here are two words that strike terror in the hearts of people trying to eat low-fat: "fried" and "nuts." But you know, I could probably eat sand off a beach if it were fried. I like serving this chicken with my Fargo Garlic Mashed Potatoes (page 162).

1½ cups low-fat buttermilk
1 tablespoon minced garlic
2 teaspoons grated fresh ginger
1 teaspoon ground cumin
1 teaspoon salt
4 chicken breast halves on the bone (about 6 ounces), skinned
½ cup dry unseasoned bread crumbs
¼ cup pecan halves, finely ground

1 In sealable plastic bag combine buttermilk, garlic, ginger, cumin, and salt. Add chicken. Shake to coat. Seal bag. Refrigerate about 8 hours or overnight, turning occasionally.

2 Preheat oven to 425°. In flat dish combine bread crumbs and ground pecans. Lift chicken pieces, one at a time, from marinade and place, meat side down, in crumbs to coat. Place, coated side up, in nonstick baking pan. Discard marinade.

3 Bake chicken, uncovered, 20 minutes. Turn oven down to 350°. Bake 15 to 20 minutes or until meat is no longer pink near bone.

NUTRIENT VALUE PER SERVING
256 calories   30 g protein
8 g fat (28% fat)   13 g carbohydrate
479 mg sodium   74 mg cholesterol

Pecans

I have a certain fondness for pecans. When I was growing up in New Orleans, I made extra money by selling homemade pecan pralines on street corners. Who said I didn't have a happy childhood? Pecans are a Sacred Fat—in fact, it's one of the fattiest nuts. Its great taste goes a long way, so you don't need much. My trick is to finely grind just a small amount (they're also expensive), and use that as a light coating for the chicken. As a result, the chicken comes in at less than 30 percent calories from fat. Where do all these sacred little nuts come from? Twenty-seven million pounds are produced in Georgia a year—that's some Sacred State.

Oven-Fried

Pan frying is something you never do if you're eating low-fat. Instead, bake with a coating and you'll get the same crunch as if it were fried.

Chicken-in-Every-Pot Pot Pie

MAKES 6 SERVINGS

Prep: 10 minutes
Stand: 20 minutes
Cook: 20 minutes
Bake: 450° for 15 to 20 minutes

Chicken pot pie is as American as apple pie. I find it everywhere, no matter where I travel in this country—even in fancy restaurants. The Pennsylvania Dutch, some say, were the first in this country to bake a chicken pie. The first versions had a double crust (or double curse), made with suet, and you know what suet is— fat! My version is, in fact, a no-crust pie. Instead, I use herbed buttermilk biscuits. You've heard of hearts and flowers? Well, this is hearts and chickens.

NUTRIENT VALUE PER SERVING
272 calories   22 g protein
6 g fat (20% fat)   33 g carbohydrate
560 mg sodium   39 mg cholesterol

FILLING

1 can (14½ ounces) fat-free reduced-sodium chicken broth
12 ounces boneless, skinned chicken breast, trimmed of all visible fat
½ cup *each* chopped onions *and* sliced leeks (white part only) *or* sliced green onions (white part only)
1 cup *each* sliced carrots *and* sliced mushrooms
½ cup evaporated skim milk
¼ cup all-purpose flour
½ teaspoon poultry seasoning mix
¼ teaspoon *each* salt *and* freshly ground black pepper
1 cup frozen peas
¼ cup chopped fresh parsley

BUTTERMILK BISCUIT TOPPING

1 cup all-purpose flour
1 teaspoon baking powder
¼ teaspoon baking soda
¼ teaspoon salt
1 tablespoon chopped fresh parsley
⅛ teaspoon poultry seasoning
2 tablespoons chilled light butter, cut into small pieces
½ cup low-fat buttermilk

1 Filling: In medium saucepan bring broth to boiling over medium-high heat. Add chicken. Cover; remove from heat. Let stand 20 minutes. Chicken will cook perfectly. Lift chicken from broth with slotted spoon; set aside.

2 To broth in saucepan add onion, leeks, and carrots. Simmer 10 minutes or until vegetables are tender. Add mushrooms. Simmer 5 minutes more.

3 Meanwhile, in screw-top jar combine evaporated skim milk, flour, poultry seasoning, salt, and pepper. Cover tightly. Shake to mix to smooth paste. Stir into vegetable mixture. Stir over medium heat until sauce thickens, 2 to 3 minutes.

4 Shred chicken into small pieces. Add with peas and parsley to thickened sauce. Set aside.

5 Preheat oven to 450°.

6 Biscuit topping: In medium bowl mix together dry ingredients with parsley and poultry seasoning.

7 Using pastry blender, 2 knives used like scissors, or fingertips, work butter into flour mixture until mixture is coarsely crumbed. Make a well in center. Pour buttermilk into well. Toss gently with fork until flour mixture is just moistened. Do not overmix. Dough will be sticky. Turn dough out onto well-floured surface. With floured hands, knead very gently once or twice to bring dough together.

8 Roll with rolling pin or lightly pat dough out to ½-inch thickness. Dip 2½-inch biscuit cutter into flour. Use to cut out biscuits. Use straight motion. Do not twist cutter. Dip cutter into flour between cuts. Gather scraps together lightly. Cut out more biscuits for a total of 6, or more than 6 if using smaller cutter.

9 Reheat chicken mixture until simmering. Immediately transfer to 2-quart casserole. Use spatula to lift biscuits on top.

10 Bake 15 to 20 minutes or until biscuits have risen and are golden brown.

$\mathcal{M}$aple-Glazed Roast Turkey Breast in a Cornbread Nest

MAKES 12 SERVINGS

Prep: 20 minutes
Cook: 8 minutes
Roast: 375° for about 2 hours
Stand: 20 minutes

Remember that song line, "How do you solve a problem like Maria?" Well, I've solved the when-do-you-stuff the bird question—you don't. No worrying about stuffing the turkey too early and getting some strange disease, or putting it in a casserole dish to bake it separately and then forgetting to put it in the oven. Instead, bake the turkey in a nest of stuffing. And no more whining about dry turkey—the glaze and the stuffing beneath keep everything moist. Thank you, Vermont, for your maple syrup.

NUTRIENT VALUE PER SERVING
(3 OUNCES MEAT, ½ CUP STUFFING)
512 calories   48 g protein
16 g fat (28% fat)   41 g carbohydrate
709 mg sodium   110 mg cholesterol

1 whole turkey breast on the bone
(6 to 6½ pounds)
1½ teaspoons *each* dried sage *and* thyme *and*
freshly ground black pepper
2 tablespoons olive oil
1¼ cups diced celery, with leaves
1 cup chopped onion
½ cup chopped fresh parsley
2 tablespoons water, or as needed
2 medium Granny Smith apples, cored
and diced (about 2½ cups)
2 bags (8 ounces *each*) cornbread stuffing
mix
1 can (14½ ounces) fat-free reduced-
sodium chicken broth

GLAZE
⅓ cup maple syrup
3 tablespoons coarse-grained Dijon-style
mustard

1 Remove skin and excess fat from turkey
breast. Rinse turkey. Blot dry with
paper towels. In cup mix sage, thyme,
and pepper. Rub 2 teaspoons over
breast.

2 Preheat oven to 375°.

3 In large nonstick skillet heat oil over
medium heat. Add celery, onion,
parsley, and remaining herb mixture.
Cook, stirring frequently, until
vegetables are slightly softened, 3 to 4
minutes. If skillet gets dry, add a
tablespoon or so of water. Stir in apples
and another tablespoon water. Cook,
stirring, 2 to 3 minutes more. Spoon

into large bowl. Add stuffing mix. In
measuring cup add enough water to
broth to equal 2¼ cups. Add to stuffing.
Toss gently to mix. Spoon into roasting
pan. If desired, place roasting rack in
pan over stuffing. Place turkey breast on
rack or directly on stuffing. Cover pan
completely with foil.

4 Roast 1½ hours.

5 In medium bowl mix glaze ingredients.
Remove foil from bird. Spoon about
one-third of glaze over breast. Roast,
uncovered, 30 to 40 minutes longer,
basting two or three times with
remaining glaze, or until instant-read
meat thermometer inserted in thickest
part of breast registers 165°. Transfer
turkey to platter and stuffing to covered
serving dish. Let turkey stand 20
minutes. Carve into thin slices.

No Cornbread in the House?

To make my life easier I use a cornbread stuffing mix
from those people who have that old-fashioned farm—
you know who I mean. But if you've had a childhood
experience that's soured you on cornbread, use other
breads: rye, sourdough, plain white that you can dry out in
the toaster oven, or anything else that strikes your fancy.

A Turkey Breast

In case you didn't notice, I use a whole turkey breast on
the bone. It's big enough for a party, a whole 6 pounds.
Since it's all white meat, it's leaner, and I've removed the
skin before roasting. If one of your dinner guests asks for
a leg, tell her you gave it to the neighbors. Plus, after
watching the movie *Tom Jones,* I just can't stand the
sight of someone eating a whole turkey.

Gonzales Chicken Jambalaya

MAKES 6 SERVINGS

Prep: 10 minutes
Cook: 35 minutes

There are some 5,000 jambalaya stories from Gonzales, Louisiana, the jambalaya capital of the world. But my favorite recipe is the one my father made. He would open the refrigerator door, grab all the leftovers—bits of chicken, shrimp, sausage, and so on—and cook it up with a lot of rice. The dish really borrows from the Asian philosophy that meat is a flavor accessory and rice is the main ingredient—which is great if you're looking to eat low-fat.

Nonstick olive oil cooking spray
¼ pound turkey link sausage
1 can (14½ ounces) fat-free sodium-reduced chicken broth
8 ounces boneless, skinned chicken breast, diced medium
1 slice (4 ounces, ¼ inch thick) Black Forest ham, diced medium
1 cup *each* chopped onion *and* green bell pepper
⅓ cup *each* chopped celery *and* green onion (green and white parts)
2 cloves garlic, chopped
1 can (15 ounces) ready-cut tomatoes
¼ cup Worcestershire sauce
2 teaspoons hot pepper sauce, *or* less for milder taste
2 teaspoons dried thyme
⅛ teaspoon *each* freshly ground black pepper *and* salt
2 tablespoons chopped fresh parsley
1½ cups uncooked white rice

1 Coat large Dutch oven with cooking spray. Heat over medium-high heat. Add sausage. Brown thoroughly, 2 to 3 minutes. Remove. Halve sausages lengthwise, then thinly slice crosswise. Return to hot pan. Stir, adding a splash of chicken broth to prevent sausage from sticking and overbrowning.

2 Add chicken. Cook, stirring frequently, 2 minutes or until lightly browned, adding more chicken broth as needed to prevent sticking and overbrowning. Add ham. Cook, stirring, 1 more minute. Remove meats. Set aside. Add splash of chicken broth to pan, stirring up any browned bits from bottom.

NUTRIENT VALUE PER SERVING
314 calories   21 g protein
4 g fat (13% fat)   47 g carbohydrate
903 mg sodium   46 mg cholesterol

Party On

A Cajun one-dish casserole meal—
great for a party. Spread the rice
mixture out on your best platter, and
top with huge baked butterflied
shrimp. The trimmings? Just a salad
and pitchers of iced tea. What could
be finer!

Seasoning Mix for All Seasons

For something special, use the
seasonings in this dish to flavor other
foods, especially quick and easy
stir-fries. Combine in a plastic food-
storage bag 2 cloves garlic, chopped,
Worcestershire sauce, hot pepper
sauce, thyme, black pepper, and salt,
and toss in chunks of chicken breast,
pork cubes, or pieces of fish and
let stand for about 30 minutes.
Then quickly stir-fry in a nonstick
skillet lightly coated with a little
nonstick cooking spray. Add a splash
of fat-free chicken broth.

3 Add onion, green pepper, celery, green onion, and
garlic. Cook, stirring, over high heat until softened,
2 to 3 minutes. Add broth as needed to prevent sticking
and overbrowning.

4 Add tomatoes and remaining chicken broth. Add all
remaining ingredients, except rice. Cover. Reduce heat
to low. Simmer 25 minutes.

5 Meanwhile, in medium saucepan cook rice according
to package directions. Stir rice into chicken mixture.
Heat through. Serve in shallow bowls.

Mr. Peanut Chicken on a Stick

Remember Mr. Peanut, that dashing fellow with the monocle and fancy cane? Well, this is his sauce, and it's a good example of how to use Sacred Fat and still have a recipe that is less than 30% calories from fat. Peanut butter — that's the culprit. Even though there are reduced-fat versions, we opted to go all the way with the full-fat. This is practically a whole meal — just add a green vegetable, such as broccoli or string beans, or a green salad.

PEANUT SAUCE

½ cup water
⅓ cup *each* rice vinegar *and* creamy-style peanut butter
2 tablespoons reduced-sodium soy sauce
1 tablespoon sugar
4 cloves garlic, peeled
2 teaspoons arrowroot
¼ to ½ teaspoon crushed red pepper flakes

12 ounces chicken tenders (see page 43)
4 cups hot cooked brown rice
Sprigs of fresh cilantro, for garnish (optional)

1 Sauce: In blender combine all ingredients for sauce. Blend until smooth. Transfer to small saucepan. Heat over medium heat, stirring constantly until heated through and thickened. Do not boil. Cool. Pour half of sauce into sealable plastic bag, setting remainder aside. Add chicken to bag. Seal and marinate in refrigerator for 1 to 2 hours. Meanwhile, soak four 6-inch bamboo skewers in water, to prevent burning during cooking.

2 Preheat broiler. Thread chicken tenders on skewers.

3 Broil skewers close to heat, 1 to 2 minutes each side or until cooked through. In small saucepan heat reserved sauce. Divide hot rice among 4 serving plates. Top with chicken. Drizzle with heated sauce, and serve extra sauce in a bowl. Garnish plates with sprigs of fresh cilantro, if desired.

NUTRIENT VALUE PER SERVING
384 calories   25 g protein
9 g fat (21% fat)   50 g carbohydrate
204 mg sodium   47 mg cholesterol

Arrowroot

You could use cornstarch for a thickener in this sauce, but I like arrowroot since it turns clear when cooked and it also has no taste—none of that chalkiness you sometimes get from undercooked cornstarch. Plus, it has about twice the thickening power of flour, so you use much less.

Other Morsels to Skewer

Cubes of pork or small pieces of turkey breast would be excellent replacements for the tenders.

Maui Turkey Kabobs

Prep: 15 minutes
Marinate: 1 hour
Broil: 8 to 10 minutes

During my career I've owned several restaurants. There's always been one I've wanted to open, called Kabobs. Twenty different kabobs—that's all I planned to serve: Roma, with sun-dried tomato and eggplant; Tokyo kabob with water chestnuts, bamboo shoots, and chicken or shrimp. I love the whole idea of a kabob— it's a culinary popsicle, a meal on a stick. Plus, in this dish, there's something very special about the combination of turkey and pineapple, especially when the pineapple gets all browned and caramelized. Thank you, Hawaii, for pineapple.

⅓ cup *each* red wine vinegar *and* bottled plum sauce
2 teaspoons reduced-sodium soy sauce
1 teaspoon *each* grated fresh ginger *and* minced garlic
1 pound turkey tenderloin steaks or cutlets
1 small zucchini
1 small yellow summer squash
1 medium red bell pepper
8 small mushrooms
8 cubes fresh *or* canned pineapple

1 In small bowl combine vinegar, plum sauce, soy sauce, ginger, and garlic. Rinse turkey and pat dry. Cut into 1-inch pieces. Place in sealable plastic bag with half the marinade. Seal bag. Refrigerate to marinate at least 1 hour, turning occasionally.

2 Cut zucchini and yellow squash into ¾-inch-thick slices. Cut red pepper into 1-inch squares. Place zucchini, squash, red pepper, mushrooms, and pineapple in separate sealable plastic bag with remainder of marinade. Seal bag. Set aside to marinate. Meanwhile, soak eight 6-inch bamboo skewers in water, to prevent burning during cooking.

3 After marinating for at least 1 hour, remove turkey and vegetables from marinade. Discard turkey marinade. Reserve vegetable marinade.

4 Remove broiler pan and preheat broiler. Thread turkey, vegetables, and pineapple on soaked skewers, intermingling colors and textures. Arrange kabobs on broiler pan.

NUTRIENT VALUE PER SERVING
169 calories   29 g protein
1 g fat (8% fat)   10 g carbohydrate
84 mg sodium   77 mg cholesterol

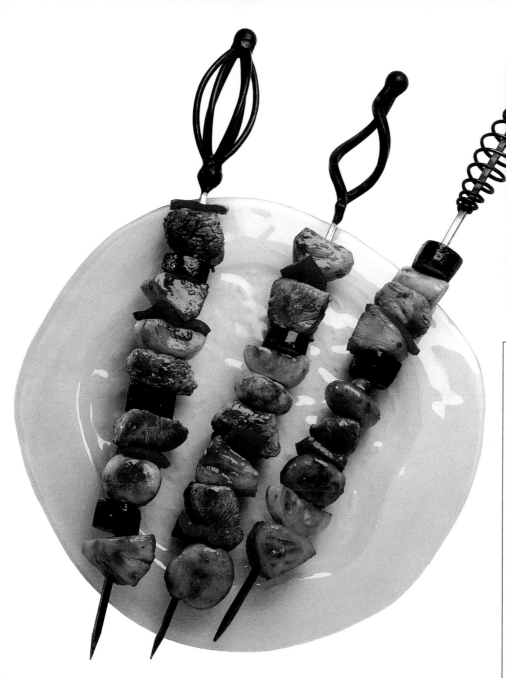

Kabob Partners

Cherry tomatoes, artichoke hearts, sweet potatoes, onions, carrots, long pieces of green onion, parsnips, turnips, beets, asparagus, eggplant, butternut or acorn squash, apples, oranges, peaches, melons, prunes—isn't that enough! Remember to keep all pieces uniform so everything is finished cooking at the same time. You may also have to precook or blanch some vegetables first, such as potatoes or carrots, to give them a head start, since the cooking time for kabobs is usually short.

Fresh Ginger

If you haven't tried fresh ginger, you're missing something. It's hotter, sweeter, and much more flavorful than the ground dried in a bottle. But watch out when you go shopping for it. It's ugly—all gnarled and bumpy. You want a piece that looks plump and with a smooth, unbroken skin. No blemishes, please. To use, cut off only as much as you need. Peel away the tan skin and mince or finely chop. Or, take a piece, unpeeled, and coarsely grate it—the skin will disappear. To store the leftover, wrap in aluminum foil, and refrigerate for up to 2 weeks, or freeze for up to a month. Delicious in marinades, stir-fries, or anywhere you want a surprising, spicy flavor.

5 Broil, 3 to 4 inches from heat source, for 5 minutes. Brush with marinade from vegetables. Turn kabobs over. Broil 3 to 5 more minutes or until turkey is no longer pink in center and vegetables are tender. Discard marinade.

Flash-in-the-Pan Turkey Cutlets

MAKES 4 SERVINGS

Prep: 15 minutes
Cook: 8 minutes

This is dinner on the run—turkey cutlets or steaks cook fast for quick dinner prep. To shave off more precious seconds from cooking time, I pound them very thin. There are different ways to pound. I have a friend who backs her Volvo up and down the driveway over the cutlets—the added bonus is a pretty diamond pattern in the meat. The easy way is the best—just put the cutlets between two sheets of wax paper and lightly bang with a rolling pin or the flat bottom of a heavy skillet.

NUTRIENT VALUE PER SERVING
263 calories   31 g protein
7 g fat (26% fat)   15 g carbohydrate
820 mg sodium   67 mg cholesterol

1 pound turkey tenderloin (thin slices
  turkey breast)
2 tablespoons Dijon-style mustard
½ cup Italian-flavored dry bread crumbs
2 tablespoons grated Parmesan cheese
1 tablespoon chopped fresh parsley
½ teaspoon *each* salt *and* salt-free
  lemon-pepper seasoning
Nonstick olive oil cooking spray
½ cup dry white wine
2 cups sliced mushrooms
12 asparagus spears, fresh *or* thawed frozen
1 tablespoon capers, rinsed and drained
  (optional)

1 Using meat mallet or bottom of
  heavy skillet or rolling pin, pound
  turkey between two pieces of wax
  paper. Spread mustard on both sides of
  each turkey slice. In plastic bag mix
  together bread crumbs, cheese, parsley,
  salt, and lemon-pepper. Add turkey.
  Shake to coat.

2 Coat large nonstick skillet with cooking
  spray. Heat over medium-high heat.
  Have wine on hand in liquid measuring
  cup. Add turkey. Cook for 30 seconds. If
  it starts to brown too quickly or stick to
  the pan, add a splash of wine (about
  2 tablespoons). Turn turkey over. Cook

on second side 30 seconds more, adding
another splash of wine.

3 Cover skillet. Remove from heat. Let
  stand 1 to 2 minutes. Remove turkey
  from pan and keep warm.

4 Lightly coat skillet again with cooking
  spray if needed. Heat skillet again over
  high heat. Add mushrooms, stirring,
  until lightly browned, 1 minute. Add
  splash of wine. Shake pan to prevent
  sticking. Add asparagus together with
  remaining wine. Cover and heat
  through, 1 to 2 minutes. Serve turkey
  with mushrooms and asparagus.
  Sprinkle with capers, if desired.

Other Coatings

For flavorful variations, pulverize in a blender or food
processor one of the following ingredients: flavored
melba toasts, low-fat tortilla chips, reduced-fat crackers,
stuffing mixes, reduced-fat low-sodium pretzels,
reduced-fat gingersnaps. Just wander your supermarket
aisles and you'll find lots of other ideas, but be sure you
don't snack your way through the market. I once did that,
and I arrived at the checkout line with an empty
shopping cart, and my clothes were covered with crumbs
and spots of salsa.

The Leaning Torta of Turkey

MAKES 6 SERVINGS
Prep: 15 minutes
Bake: 350° for 15 minutes

Keep stacking the layers of this torta up, higher and higher, and you'll quickly know why I call this the leaning tower of torta. My torta speaks Spanish since it uses ingredients that have migrated across the border from Mexico to our Southwest.

Tomatillo

When you see one of these fresh, you'll know why it's called the Mexican green tomato. It's related to the tomato—a little smaller, with a papery outer skin. The taste is a combination of lemon, apple, and herbs. To make it easier, this recipe uses a canned tomatillo sauce.

NUTRIENT VALUE PER SERVING
319 calories   18 g protein
14 g fat (39% fat)   30 g carbohydrate
529 mg sodium   57 mg cholesterol

8 ounces ground turkey
1 clove garlic, minced
½ teaspoon salt-free Mexican seasoning

GREEN SAUCE
¼ cup diced onion
¼ cup chopped fresh cilantro
1 small can (7 ounces) tomatillo sauce
Pinch of salt

1 can (15 ounces) black beans, drained and rinsed
1 can (10 ounces) mild enchilada sauce
5 corn tortillas (5 to 6 inches each)
½ cup bottled red salsa
3 ounces reduced-fat Monterey Jack cheese, shredded
Fresh cilantro sprigs, for garnish

1 Preheat oven to 350°. Line 9-inch pie plate with foil.

2 Heat nonstick skillet over medium-high heat. Add ground turkey, garlic, and Mexican seasoning. Cook, stirring, until turkey is browned and crumbly, 4 to 5 minutes. Drain off any fat. Set turkey aside.

3 Green Sauce: In blender or small food processor combine onion, cilantro, tomatillo sauce, and salt. Process until smooth. Scrape into small bowl. Rinse out blender or processor container; puree beans.

4 Assemble torta: In medium saucepan warm enchilada sauce. Dip tortillas quickly in and out of sauce. Place 1 tortilla in prepared pie plate. Layer with one quarter *each* of pureed beans, turkey mixture, green sauce, red salsa, and cheese. Repeat 3 more layers, reserving a

sprinkling of cheese. End with tortilla on top. Cover with remaining enchilada sauce. Sprinkle with remaining cheese.

5 Bake 15 minutes or until heated through. Garnish with cilantro sprigs. Cut into wedges to serve.

It's a Party!

Make two of these—the second with ground chicken or very lean ground beef, or roasted sliced vegetables (see Que Sera Quesadilla with Vegetables, page 23).

Sacred Fat

It's the cheese—that's the Sacred Fat. So even though this recipe weighs in at 39 percent calories from fat, the calories are low and the actual grams of fat are not astronomical. Plus, remember, this is a complete meal in itself. Add a green salad and the numbers will improve.

$\mathcal{P}$uff, the Magic Meal

MAKES 6 SERVINGS

Prep: 10 minutes
Cook: 35 minutes
Bake: 425° for 30 minutes

Some of you may remember a dish from the 1950s and '60s called the "impossible meal." The secret ingredient was a box of biscuit mix. This is my updated version that uses—are you ready?—Yorkshire pudding. It's stately, and delicious. And although I use ground turkey, there's only about 3 ounces per person.

Sacred Fat

Two whole eggs—what could be more sacred than that! And I don't stop there. There's cheese, two kinds, and even light butter. It's the impossible dream, almost come true.

NUTRIENT VALUE PER SERVING
310 calories   24 g protein
12 g fat (36% fat)   25 g carbohydrate
691 mg sodium   131 mg cholesterol

Nonstick olive oil cooking spray

- 1 cup finely chopped onion
- 1 teaspoon fresh minced garlic
- 2 cups Japanese eggplant, unpeeled, cut in fourths lengthwise, then cut crosswise into small chunks
- 1 pound lean ground turkey
- 1 teaspoon dried basil
- ½ teaspoon *each* dried oregano *and* ground cinnamon *and* salt
- ¼ teaspoon freshly ground black pepper
- 1 can (8 ounces) tomato sauce
- 1 tablespoon light butter

YORKSHIRE PUDDING

- 2 large eggs
- 1 cup skim milk
- 1 cup all-purpose flour
- ¼ teaspoon salt
- ¼ cup shredded reduced-fat sharp cheddar cheese
- 2 tablespoons grated Parmesan cheese

1 Coat large nonstick skillet with cooking spray. Heat over medium-high heat. Add onion, garlic, and eggplant. Cook, stirring constantly, 5 to 7 minutes or until onion is softened and eggplant is golden brown. Remove vegetables from skillet and set aside.

2 Recoat skillet with cooking spray. Heat over medium-high heat. Add turkey. Cook over medium heat, stirring constantly, until no longer pink, 3 minutes. Add basil, oregano, cinnamon, salt, and pepper. Stir in tomato sauce and reserved eggplant mixture. Bring to a boil. Reduce heat and simmer, covered, 20 minutes, stirring occasionally.

3 Preheat oven to 425°. Place butter in 10-inch pie plate. Place in oven until butter is melted.

4 Yorkshire Pudding: In medium bowl beat eggs lightly. Add milk. Beat until well blended. Add flour and salt. Beat until batter is smooth. Pour batter into heated pie plate. Place turkey mixture in middle of batter. Spread out to within 1 inch of edge. Sprinkle with cheddar and Parmesan cheeses.

5 Bake 30 minutes or until brown and puffy. Cut in wedges and serve.

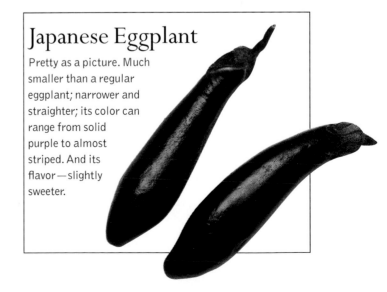

Japanese Eggplant

Pretty as a picture. Much smaller than a regular eggplant; narrower and straighter; its color can range from solid purple to almost striped. And its flavor—slightly sweeter.

Spiral Loaf, Nicknamed Meatloaf

MAKES 8 SERVINGS

Prep: 25 minutes
Bake: 350° for 55 minutes

Say meatloaf (or meatball), and lots of people will turn their heads because that's their nickname. But say meatloaf and mashed potatoes, and that's diner food, a comfort meal. Even though meatloaf has been with us forever, it's now enjoying a huge comeback, appearing on restaurant menus everywhere. But you know, in my travels it always looks the same — a loaf of bread with ketchup on top. Not mine — this is a party dish with lots of color. And leftovers, if there are any, are great in sandwiches. Cold meatloaf sandwiches! The only thing better is a cold turkey stuffing sandwich!

1 pound extra-lean ground beef
1½ cups fresh bread crumbs
2 large egg whites
⅓ cup *each* chopped onion *and* chopped celery *and* chopped fresh parsley
½ teaspoon salt
¼ teaspoon freshly ground black pepper
1 can (5.5 ounces) mixed vegetable juice
1 tablespoon Worcestershire sauce
1 tablespoon country-style Dijon-style mustard
1 package (10 ounces) frozen chopped spinach, thawed and squeezed dry
1 teaspoon salt-free herb seasoning
4 ounces very thinly sliced part-skim mozzarella cheese
4 red bell peppers, roasted, cored, seeded, and peeled (see page 18) *or* 6 jarred roasted red bell peppers, seeds removed
1 teaspoon salt-free garlic-herb seasoning

1 Preheat oven to 350°.

2 In large bowl combine beef, bread crumbs, egg whites, onion, celery, parsley, salt, pepper, vegetable juice, Worcestershire sauce, and mustard.

3 On sheet of foil or wax paper, shape meat into 14 x 10-inch rectangle. Cover surface with thawed spinach. Sprinkle with herb seasoning. Layer mozzarella slices over top. Cover with roasted peppers. Sprinkle with garlic-herb seasoning.

NUTRIENT VALUE PER SERVING
201 calories   19 g protein
9 g fat (41% fat)   11 g carbohydrate
479 mg sodium   48 mg cholesterol

Get a Jump

You can assemble this earlier in the day, wrap it in plastic wrap, and refrigerate. Then pop it in the oven just before the guests arrive. If it's going directly from the refrigerator to the oven, allow a little extra baking time.

Part of a Meal

Here's a nutrition lesson: Notice that the meatloaf racks in at 41 percent calories from fat, but a serving contains only 9 grams of fat, plus the calories are low. Put this in a context of a whole meal and see what happens: Serve each portion with 1 cup cooked carrots and 1 serving Fargo Garlic Mashed Potatoes, page 162. The nutrition results, for the whole meal: 397 calories, 23 g protein, 15 g fat (33%), 44 g carbohydrate, 683 mg sodium, 49 mg cholesterol. Not bad for meatloaf. Remember, there are times when you need a little Sacred Fat to make life worth living. Here, it's ground beef and part-skim mozzarella. Just be sure to balance it out during the rest of the day. If you want to drop the fat a little, substitute ground turkey for the ground beef.

4 Starting at a short side, roll up meatloaf to enclose filling, using foil or paper as a guide. Place loaf, seam side down, in rectangular nonstick baking pan. Tent loosely with aluminum foil.

5 Bake meatloaf 35 minutes. Remove foil. Bake, uncovered, 20 minutes more or until juices run clear. Let meat loaf stand 5 to 10 minutes before slicing.

Nonfat Flavor Boost

Just a little can of mixed vegetable juice (actually it's V-8, but I don't want to plug any products), is a great nonfat way to punch up flavor.

South Fork Beef Stew

MAKES 4 SERVINGS

Prep: 25 minutes
Cook: 1 hour 10 minutes

I can see it now—cowboys cooking pots of beef stew during those long nights on the prairie; coyotes howling at the moon. That's my inspiration for this recipe. Do you think I watched too much *Bonanza* and *Rawhide* when I was growing up?

Color Me Brown

Beef stew was such a ritual in my house. I can remember my father carefully cubing the meat and dusting it with flour—me singing all the while, "You don't dip me in flour anymore, anymore." That was the secret—the flour, not my singing. The meat turned a rich brown as it cooked in the hot skillet, and the flour helped seal in the juices as well as thickening the stew.

NUTRIENT VALUE PER SERVING

335 calories   27 g protein
8 g fat (22% fat)   28 g carbohydrate
926 mg sodium   70 mg cholesterol

¼   cup all-purpose flour
½   teaspoon freshly ground black pepper
1   pound extra-lean stew beef, trimmed of all visible fat and cut into ¾-inch cubes
Nonstick olive oil cooking spray
1   cup dry red wine
1   cup *each* small pearl onions *and* sliced carrots *and* cubed, peeled potatoes
2   cloves garlic, chopped
1   bay leaf
¼   teaspoon dried thyme
1   can (14½ ounces) beef broth
1½ cups sliced mushrooms
½   cup frozen green peas
2   tablespoons cornstarch (optional)
¼   teaspoon salt
Fresh thyme sprigs, for garnish (optional)

1 In medium bowl combine flour and ¼ teaspoon pepper. Using clean hands, add beef and toss to thoroughly coat with seasoned flour. Shake off any excess flour.

2 Coat large nonstick saucepan with cooking spray. Heat over medium-high heat. Add half the meat. Cook, stirring constantly, 5 minutes or until meat is browned. Remove browned meat and set aside. Coat same pan with more cooking spray. Brown remaining meat. Leave in pan.

3 To pan, add a little of the wine. Stir with wooden spoon to loosen any browned bits stuck to bottom. Then return first batch of browned meat to second batch in

saucepan. Add onions, carrot, potato, garlic, bay leaf, thyme, remaining wine, and beef broth.

4 Partially cover. Bring to boil over medium heat. Simmer gently over low heat about 50 minutes or until meat is tender when pierced with fork.

5 Add mushrooms. Cook 5 minutes. Add peas. Cook 5 minutes more.

6 If you want thicker gravy, spoon out a little of the broth into small bowl. Add cornstarch and stir to dissolve. Add cornstarch mixture to stew. Stir over medium heat until gravy thickens. Add salt and remaining ¼ teaspoon pepper. Remove and discard bay leaf. Garnish with fresh thyme, if desired.

Hi, Mr. Butcher

If you haven't met, by all means introduce yourself. "Hi, are you the head butcher? My rising sign is lamb. What's yours? I'm having Mother Teresa over tonight for beef stew. Can you suggest a lean cut of beef for stew — you know how Mother watches her weight — and is there anything on special?" Isn't that easy? Feel free to substitute your own favorite personality for Mother Teresa. You could even use my name! The leaner cuts that I use for my stew are bottom round or a round tip roast. Remember, lean means less fat.

$\mathcal{S}$wanky Flanky Steak

MAKES 4 SERVINGS

Prep: 10 minutes
Marinate: 1 to 8 hours
Broil: 6 to 8 minutes
Stand: 10 minutes

This recipe does double duty—it's like bonus coupons. You can serve the flank steak as is, dressed up with vegetables, or turn to my recipe for Philadelphia Cheese Steak Sandwich (page 63). Flank steak was always cheap, because it's a tough, thin, stringy cut of beef. And the name wasn't all that attractive, either. So someone invented the name London Broil, and the price went up. Just goes to show you that a flank steak by any other name is a rose.

NUTRIENT VALUE PER SERVING
204 calories   23 g protein
11 g fat (50% fat)   1 g carbohydrate
191 mg sodium   59 mg cholesterol

MARINADE

- 1 can (14½ ounces) beef broth
- ⅓ cup *each* balsamic vinegar *and* reduced-sodium soy sauce
- ½ cup finely chopped onion
- 3 cloves garlic, finely chopped
- 3 tablespoons Dijon-style mustard with horseradish
- 1 tablespoon Worcestershire sauce
- 1 bay leaf
- 1 teaspoon dried basil
- ½ teaspoon *each* dried oregano *and* dried thyme *and* dried sage
- ¼ teaspoon freshly ground black pepper

- 1 pound flank steak

1 Marinade: Combine all marinade ingredients in sealable plastic food-storage bag. Seal and shake to mix. Place steak in bag. Shake and mix. Place in refrigerator and let marinate 1 to 8 hours.

2 Preheat broiler. Lift meat from marinade. Discard marinade. Place meat on broiler-pan rack.

3 Broil steak, 5 to 6 inches from heat source, about 3 minutes per side (rare) or 4 minutes per side (medium).

4 Remove meat to cutting board. Let stand 10 minutes. Thinly slice across grain on a diagonal.

Untoughening the Tough

Here are two good techniques to know about. First, marinating helps break down fiber for more tender beef. The acid in the marinade, whether vinegar, soy sauce, lemon juice, or wine is what does it. And remember, if you have any aluminum pots without a lining left in your cupboard, don't use them—the acid will react with the aluminum for some very strange color and taste results. The second technique. Slicing the meat very, very, very thin at a 45 degree angle, makes for tender slices.

Nutrition Lesson!

When the flank steak is combined with boiled potatoes and spinach, the nutrition radically changes. And remember, this is the main meal of the day: 357 calories, 33 g protein, 12 g fat (29%), 30 g carbohydrate, 322 mg sodium, 30 mg cholesterol. See how that percentage of fat changes?

$\mathcal{M}$ayflower Shepherd's Pie

MAKES 4 SERVINGS

Prep: 15 minutes
Cook: 20 minutes
Bake: 450° for 15 minutes

Leftovers are an American tradition, and you don't get more traditional than this. (Actually the pie is British, but it crossed the Atlantic in steerage class aboard the Mayflower.) I've added my own decorative touches—doesn't even look like a pie now.

Sacred Fat

Ground beef—that's my SF here. Even though the percentage of calories from fat is above 30 percent, the calories and actual grams of fat are within reason. And this is the whole meal, vegetables and all.

NUTRIENT VALUE PER SERVING
375 calories   28 g protein
16 g fat (38% fat)   30 g carbohydrate
968 mg sodium   77 mg cholesterol

1 pound extra-lean ground beef *or* turkey
Nonstick olive oil cooking spray
1 cup chopped onion
1 large clove garlic, finely chopped
½ cup sliced carrots
1 can (14½ ounces) beef broth
1 cup sliced mushrooms
½ cup frozen peas
2 tablespoons cornstarch
1 can (5.5 ounces) mixed vegetable juice
2 teaspoons Worcestershire sauce
½ teaspoon dried rosemary
¼ teaspoon *each* salt *and* freshly ground
   black pepper
2 cups Fargo Garlic Mashed Potatoes
   (page 162)
1 tablespoon grated Parmesan cheese

1 Heat large nonstick skillet over medium heat. Add ground meat. Cook, stirring, until browned and crumbly, 4 to 6 minutes. Remove meat with slotted spoon to colander to drain. Drain any fat from skillet.

2 Coat same skillet with cooking spray. Add onion, garlic, and carrots. Cook, stirring, about 2 minutes or until onion is softened, adding a little beef broth to prevent sticking and overbrowning as needed.

3 Add remaining broth. Bring to boil. Reduce heat. Cover and simmer for 5 minutes or until vegetables are just tender.

4 Add mushrooms and peas. Cook 1 minute more.

5 Preheat oven to 450°.

6 In small bowl stir cornstarch into mixed vegetable juice to dissolve. Add to cooked vegetables. Stir over medium heat until mixture thickens, about 2 minutes. Add Worcestershire, rosemary, salt, pepper, and browned meat. Transfer mixture to 2-quart casserole.

7 Spread mashed potatoes over top of pie, or spoon on dollops of mashed potatoes. Swirl with fork to decorate. Sprinkle potatoes with Parmesan.

8 Bake 15 minutes or until potato topping is golden brown and filling is bubbly.

Note: Any leftover cooked meat you may have can be chopped or ground, and used instead of the uncooked ground meat called for in the recipe. Start recipe with step 2.

Party Toppings

Take a plastic food-storage bag, and spoon in the mashed potatoes. Snip off one corner, then pipe out the potatoes in star- or heart-shaped designs, or use a decorative star tip. For something more technicolor, spread the potatoes as described in the recipe. Then create a picture with blanched vegetables over the potatoes: for example, green beans for rolling wheat fields, and a very thin carrot slice for the sun. At holiday time, create a nativity scene, complete with shepherds.

French Quarter Red Beans and Rice

MAKES 4 SERVINGS

Soak: overnight
Prep: 15 minutes
Cook: 3½ hours

In many homes mashed potatoes and gravy or spaghetti and meatballs are the staples. Not so in many parts of the South where it's red beans and rice. Originally this was a dish served on Mondays, using the leftovers from Sunday's ham. There are almost as many variations as there are cooks—but this is my favorite.

NUTRIENT VALUE PER SERVING
381 calories   26 g protein
2 g fat (5% fat)   67 g carbohydrate
916 mg sodium   16 mg cholesterol

2 cups dried red beans
6½ cups water
1 cup chopped onion
¾ cup diced celery, including tops and leaves
½ cup diced green bell pepper
1 cup sliced carrots
4 ounces Black Forest *or* baked Virginia ham, cubed
½ teaspoon dried thyme
4 cloves garlic, minced
2 to 3 teaspoons green hot sauce
1 teaspoon salt
1½ cups uncooked white rice

1 In large bowl combine beans in enough cold water to cover by 2 inches. Let stand at cool room temperature overnight. Drain.

2 In large Dutch oven or saucepan combine drained beans, 6 cups water, onion, celery, pepper, carrot, ham, thyme, and garlic. Reduce heat. Simmer, uncovered, stirring occasionally, 3 hours. Add more water as necessary if mixture begins to look dry.

3 Stir in remaining ½ cup water, the hot sauce, and salt. Simmer 30 minutes.

4 Meanwhile, cook rice according to package directions.

5 Serve beans over hot rice.

Complementary Protein

An important point, without going into a lot of technical stuff: rice and beans, or legumes, combine to provide all the essential amino acids you need to keep the body working and growing, without extra fat and cholesterol. Remember, this is a nonanimal source of protein, so none of those nasties to worry about. In this recipe, I use the ham just as a flavoring—only 1 ounce per person. Not like when I was growing up and we just poured bacon grease over the whole thing—made me real glossy, especially after I had three bowls of it.

How I Ate Red Beans and Rice

When my father made this at home, he liked to shred the pork rather than cubing it—this made the bean mixture much thicker. But the best part, I remember, is what I put on top: first, lots of chopped onion, and then ketchup, as much as I wanted. O.K., O.K., there was more—I'm not going to lie to you. I did finally add a pile of cheddar cheese. There it is—I've spilled the beans.

Sunshine Stuffed Pork Chops

Prep: 10 minutes
Bake: 325° for 35 minutes

This recipe has a triple hit of sunny orange flavor—orange zest, orange juice, and orange marmalade. That's why I call them sunshine chops. So if it's a gray day and you're feeling gloomy, just let the sun shine in—think of me and fix these pork chops. But be warned: You'll need sunglasses.

1 clove garlic, peeled and cut in half
4 center-cut loin pork chops on the bone (about 6 ounces each), trimmed of all visible fat
½ teaspoon *each* freshly ground black pepper *and* paprika
Nonstick olive oil cooking spray
¼ cup orange marmalade
1 can (14½ ounces) fat-free reduced-sodium chicken broth
½ cup finely diced onion
2 tablespoons grated orange zest
¼ teaspoon salt
¼ cup fresh squeezed orange juice
1 cup uncooked white rice (not converted)

1 Preheat oven to 325°. Rub garlic all over chops. Discard garlic. In small cup, mix pepper and paprika. Rub all over chops.

2 Coat large ovenproof skillet with cooking spray. Heat over medium-high heat. Add pork chops. Cook 1 minute per side or until browned.

3 Remove chops from pan. Spread marmalade on one side of each chop. Set aside.

4 Add broth to skillet and heat. Add onion, orange zest, and salt. When mixture comes to a boil, add orange juice and rice. Cover.

5 Bake rice in oven 10 minutes.

NUTRIENT VALUE PER SERVING
420 calories   30 g protein
8 g fat (17% fat)   55 g carbohydrate
334 mg sodium   75 mg cholesterol

6 Place pork chops, marmalade side up, on top of rice. Cover and bake about another 25 minutes or until rice is tender, liquid has been absorbed, and chops are cooked through.

The Alternative White Meat

Mention white meat and we always think of chicken breast, white and lean. But pork is now the alternative white meat. It's bred very lean these days, so it easily fits into a low-fat eating plan, in moderation. Keep those serving sizes at 3 ounces or less. (In this recipe, once you discount the bone and trimmed fat, the serving size of meat will be about 3 ounces.)

Rice is Nice

Other rices that would be good in this dish are some of the aromatic rices, such as basmati or Texmati or pecan. They have a wonderfully nutty, almost sweet flavor that is terrific with the pork chops and orange. Just cruise the rice section of your supermarket to check out the wide assortment now available. Be sure to read the labels for cooking times, since some of these may take a little longer than ordinary white rice. If they do, just increase the initial rice cooking time in the recipe.

Cabbage Rolls with I-Don't-Hate-Sauerkraut Anymore

MAKES 4 SERVINGS
(3 ROLLS EACH)

Prep: 20 minutes
Cook: 20 minutes
Bake: 375° for 45 minutes

Before you turn your nose up at even the mention of sauerkraut, stop right now. I use just a little in this dish—it hides in the filling among the golden raisins and rice, adding a delicious flavor accent. The turkey sausage adds even more flavor, without a lot of extra fat. And you know what? This portion size is huge—you get three of the cabbage rolls.

NUTRIENT VALUE PER SERVING
(3 ROLLS)
267 calories   15 g protein
5 g fat (17% fat)   44 g carbohydrate
841 mg sodium   34 mg cholesterol

12 unblemished leaves of head of green cabbage
 6 ounces hot Italian turkey sausage, casing removed
 2 to 3 tablespoons water, if needed
 ½ cup thinly sliced green onion (green and white parts)
1½ cups cooked white rice
 ⅓ cup sauerkraut, rinsed, drained, and squeezed dry
 2 large egg whites
 ¼ cup golden raisins
 1 can (14½ ounces) stewed tomatoes, coarsely chopped
 ¼ cup tomato paste

1 Bring large pot of water to boil. Add cabbage leaves, 2 or 3 at a time. Press down into water with wooden spoon. Cook 2 to 3 minutes or until pliable. Remove with tongs to colander. Cool under cold tap water. Drain between sheets of paper towel. Repeat with remaining leaves.

2 In large nonstick skillet place sausage with 1 tablespoon water. Cook over medium heat, 6 to 8 minutes or until cooked through, breaking up sausage into chunks with wooden spoon. If skillet gets dry, add another tablespoon water. Stir in green onion and 1 more tablespoon water. Cook, stirring, 1 minute or until green onion is softened. Transfer mixture to medium bowl. When cool enough to handle, crumble sausage as finely as possible.

3 Add cooked rice, sauerkraut, egg whites, raisins, and ¼ cup stewed tomatoes to sausage mixture.

4 Preheat oven to 375°.

5 From bottom of one prepared cabbage
leaf, cut out thick part of core. Trim end
straight. Spoon about 3 tablespoons of
filling on lower half of leaf. Fold end of
leaf over filling. Fold sides over and roll
leaf up firmly. If leaf is very large, trim
off some of top. Place roll, seam side
down, in 11 x 7-inch baking dish.
Repeat with remaining leaves and filling.

6 In small bowl combine remaining
stewed tomatoes and tomato paste.
Pour over cabbage rolls. Cover dish with
aluminum foil.

7 Bake 45 minutes or until bubbly and
rolls are tender when poked with fork.

Harvest-Time Stuffed Peppers

MAKES 4 SERVINGS

Prep: 15 minutes
Cook: 5 minutes
Bake: 375° for 45 minutes

Y[Y]ou're not going to believe how rich and delicious these stuffed peppers are. The secret is grated Parmesan and a dollop of fat-free sour cream mixed in with the brown rice filling (plus some Sacred Fat). Brown rice, that's right. Don't get nervous on me — we're not talking Sixties cardboard-tasting health food. Brown rice gives extra fiber and vitamins and minerals and a wonderful nutty flavor. Unlike many stuffed pepper recipes, I don't blanch the peppers first — so one less cooking step. These roast nicely as they cook.

4 large red *or* yellow *or* green bell peppers
  (*or* a combination of them)
Nonstick vegetable oil cooking spray
1 cup sweet corn kernels, frozen *or* canned
2 tablespoons pine nuts
⅔ cup chopped green onions (green and white parts)
2 cups cooked brown rice
2 slices bacon, cooked crisp and crumbled
½ cup grated Parmesan cheese
2 tablespoons fat-free sour cream
1 tablespoon Worcestershire sauce
1 teaspoon minced garlic
½ teaspoon salt
¼ teaspoon thyme
⅛ teaspoon *each* freshly ground black pepper *and* celery
  seed, crushed

1 Preheat oven to 375°. Cut peppers in half lengthwise. Remove seeds and ribs.

2 Coat nonstick skillet with cooking spray. Heat over medium-high heat. Add corn and pine nuts. Cook, stirring, until corn starts to brown and pop and pine nuts are toasted, about 4 minutes. Add green onion. Cook, stirring, 1 minute more. Remove from heat.

3 In medium bowl combine corn mixture, rice, bacon, half of Parmesan cheese, sour cream, Worcestershire sauce, garlic, salt, thyme, pepper, and celery seed. Stir gently to mix. Divide mixture evenly among pepper halves, pressing stuffing down lightly. Arrange peppers

NUTRIENT VALUE PER SERVING
272 calories   12 g protein
8 g fat (26% fat)   40 g carbohydrate
597 mg sodium   13 mg cholesterol

in 13 x 9 x 2-inch baking pan. Pour
½ cup of hot water around peppers.
Cover loosely with foil.

4 Bake 30 minutes. Remove foil. Sprinkle
peppers with remaining cheese. Bake,
uncovered, 15 minutes. Serve warm.

Couch-Potato Peppers

Most stuffed peppers stand up with their little hats on.
Not mine. I cut them in half lengthwise, so they can
recline. They're easier to eat and prettier to look at.

Sacred Fat: Bacon and Pine Nuts

When you weren't looking,
I sneaked in a little fat, just
for flavor: two slices of bacon
and pine nuts (also called
pignoli). Pine nuts actually
come from pine cones. They're
used in classic Italian basil pesto.
To keep the nuts from going rancid
(since they do contain fat) keep them
refrigerated, for up to 3 months; or even better,
you can freeze them for up to 9 months.

Double-Surprise Lamb Chops

I love surprises in my food, and this has two. First, it's got the fastest marinade in the west. Just plain old lemon juice, and all it takes is 10 minutes to soak the chops with flavor. Second surprise—a very light bread crumb–feta cheese stuffing, hidden in a pocket. If you haven't noticed, the flavorings in this dish are Greek-inspired: lemon, feta, rosemary, and of course the lamb.

4 center-cut loin lamb chops (about 4 ounces each), trimmed of all visible fat
2 cloves garlic, peeled and cut in half
¼ cup fresh lemon juice
2 tablespoons crumbled feta cheese
1 tablespoon unseasoned dry bread crumbs
1 teaspoon dried rosemary, finely chopped
4 cups hot cooked orzo *or* white *or* brown rice cooked in fat-free chicken broth
Lemon zest *and* sprigs of rosemary, for garnish

1 Cut slit into side of each lamb chop to form pocket. Rub chops all over with cut sides of garlic. Cut second slit next to bone in each chop and insert garlic half.

2 In sealable plastic food-storage bag, combine lamb chops and lemon juice. Seal and marinate chops for 10 minutes, turning occasionally.

3 In small bowl combine feta, bread crumbs, and rosemary.

4 Preheat broiler. Remove chops from marinade. Stuff each pocket with feta mixture. Place chops on broiler-pan rack.

5 Broil chops about 2 inches from heat source for 4 minutes on one side. Turn chops over and broil 3 minutes on other side (medium-rare) or until desired doneness.

6 Serve lamb chops with orzo or rice. Garnish each chop with lemon zest and sprig of rosemary.

NUTRIENT VALUE PER SERVING
202 calories   18 g protein
6 g fat (27% fat)   18 g carbohydrate
521 mg sodium   51 mg cholesterol

Feta Cheese

This is a crumbly cheese made in a salty brine with sheep's or goat's milk A little goes a long way since it's strongly flavored, so there's less of a chance of loading up on fat. You've probably seen it crumbled over Greek salads and in pita pocket sandwiches — there's that pocket again.

Orzo

Tired of rice? Try this. Orzo is a rice-shaped pasta that cooks up just like rice, but with a very rich, creamy texture that makes you think you're in the middle of a fat indulgence.

Exotic Seattle Salmon

MAKES 4 SERVINGS

Prep: 15 minutes
Bake: 425° for 10 to 15 minutes

The Pacific Northwest is big salmon country—and salmon is one of my favorite fish. I love walking through the Pike Place Market in Seattle and looking at all the fresh fish, gorgeously displayed on beds of crushed ice. I remember years ago salmon was always served with Béarnaise sauce. You know what that is: butter, butter, and more butter, with a little egg yolk thrown in. Ouch! Not this recipe. Here I incorporate some Asian flavors to keep the dish low-fat.

NUTRIENT VALUE PER SERVING
171 calories   23 g protein
8 g fat (42% fat)   1 g carbohydrate
223 mg sodium   64 mg cholesterol

2 tablespoons rice wine vinegar
2 tablespoons teriyaki sauce
½ teaspoon dark sesame oil
¼ teaspoon chili oil
1 pound salmon fillets

1 Preheat oven to 425°. In small bowl combine vinegar, teriyaki sauce, sesame oil, and chili oil. Place salmon in glass baking dish. Pour teriyaki mixture over salmon. Let stand 10 minutes.

2 Bake, basting with pan juices once or twice, 10 to 15 minutes, depending on thickness of fish, until opaque in center. Serve with couscous and snow peas.

Omega-3 Oils and Other Nutritional Thoughts

Remember that salmon is a fatty fish, but it is high in Omega-3 oils, a kind of polyunsaturated fat that is thought to reduce the risk of coronary disease. You'll notice that the percentage of calories from fat for this recipe is more than 30 percent, but the actual number of grams of fat is low, only 8. And look at the calories: 171, which is practically nothing. When the calories are low, the percentage will often be higher than 30 percent. But when the salmon becomes part of the whole meal, the percentage drops to 19 percent (see Buddies on the Plate, this page). That's an important lesson to remember: You really need to look at what you eat during the whole day. The goal is keep the average at less than 30 percent.

Asian Flavors

Dark Asian or Oriental **sesame oil** is a heavy oil used in small quantities to flavor foods with the taste of toasted sesame seeds. **Rice** or **rice-wine vinegar** is sweeter than most other vinegars, with much less acidity. **Chili oil** is vegetable oil in which fiery red chili peppers have been steeped— a little goes a long way.

Buddies on the Plate

I like to serve the salmon with couscous (page 49), which is small granules of semolina. It's very easy to make—you just pour a hot liquid over it and let it steep for about 5 minutes. Figure on 1 cup cooked couscous for each serving. Blanched snow peas add a little forest of green to the plate—½ cup lightly cooked, per serving is fine.

Chesapeake Bay Crab Cakes with Tarragon Sauce

Prep: 20 minutes
Cook: 16 minutes

I've had crab cakes 150 different ways. Growing up, I thought crab cakes were just an excuse for having mounds of tartar sauce — the cakes were the garnish. Did you know that crab is the second most popular shellfish, after shrimp? It comes canned, frozen, and fresh. Just mention Chesapeake Bay, and most people's eyes glaze with visions of steamed crabs, crab boils, crab cakes, and heaps of shells on newspapers after a major feed.

TARRAGON SAUCE

¼ cup reduced-fat mayonnaise
¼ cup sweet pickle relish
2 tablespoons *each* skim milk *and* Dijon-style mustard
1 tablespoon chopped fresh tarragon *or* 1 teaspoon dried
1 tablespoon chopped fresh parsley

CRAB CAKES

16 ounces canned crabmeat *or* fresh lump crabmeat
¼ cup reduced-fat mayonnaise
½ cup unseasoned dry bread crumbs
¼ cup finely chopped green onion (green and white parts)
1 tablespoon Dijon-style mustard
1 large egg white
4 drops hot pepper sauce
Nonstick vegetable oil cooking spray

1 Sauce: In small bowl combine mayonnaise, relish, milk, mustard, tarragon, and parsley. Cover and refrigerate until ready to use.

2 Crab cakes: In medium bowl combine crabmeat, mayonnaise, ¼ cup bread crumbs, green onion, mustard, egg white, and pepper sauce just until blended. Shape into eight 3-inch patties. Dip each into remaining bread crumbs to coat.

3 Coat large nonstick skillet with cooking spray. Heat over medium-high heat. Cook crab cakes, in two batches, about 4 minutes per side or until golden. Serve with sauce.

NUTRIENT VALUE PER SERVING
129 calories   14 protein
3 g fat (19% fat)   12 g carbohydrate
591 mg sodium   51 mg cholesterol

all River Baked Flounder

MAKES 4 SERVINGS

Prep: 15 minutes
Cook: 2 minutes
Bake: 450° for 20 minutes

When I saw my first live flounder at the aquarium, I turned to my mother and said, "Where's the batter?" I had never seen a fish that wasn't deep-fried. My recipe here puts bread crumbs inside the fish, in a luscious stuffing. Be sure to eat it slowly; you could easily eat all four portions before you realize it. This recipe is based on one I had in a fish shack restaurant in Fall River, Massachusetts—spotlessly clean linoleum floors and plastic drinking glasses, and fish that was about five minutes out of the water.

NUTRIENT VALUE PER SERVING
162 calories   21 g protein
2 g fat (12% fat)   13 g carbohydrate
464 mg sodium   53 mg cholesterol

Nonstick vegetable oil cooking spray
¼ cup finely chopped onion
1 clove garlic, minced
2 teaspoons grated lemon zest
½ cup chopped fresh mushrooms
¼ cup shredded carrot
½ cup unseasoned dry bread crumbs
½ cup chopped fresh parsley
1 tablespoon fresh lemon juice
½ teaspoon salt
¼ teaspoon freshly ground black pepper
4 flounder fillets (about 4 ounces *each*) or
  8 Dover sole fillets (about 2 ounces *each*)
¼ cup dry white wine
1 teaspoon paprika

1 Coat nonstick medium skillet with cooking spray. Heat over medium-high heat. Add onion, garlic, and lemon zest. Cook, stirring, about 30 seconds. Add mushrooms and carrot. Cook, stirring, about 1 minute or until juice released from mushrooms has almost evaporated.

2 Stir in bread crumbs, ⅓ cup of the parsley, lemon juice, salt, and pepper. Remove from heat.

3 Preheat oven to 450°. Lay flounder or sole fillets, skinned side up, on work surface. Spread stuffing lengthwise along each fillet, dividing equally. Roll up fillets from one end to the other. Place, seam side down, in shallow baking dish. Pour wine over fish. Sprinkle with paprika.

4 Bake, basting fish occasionally with pan liquid, about 20 minutes or until stuffing is heated through and fish is opaque. Garnish with remaining chopped parsley.

Mushrooms—Other Than Canned

We all know what the white button variety of mushroom looks like, but take another look in the produce section and you'll discover other kinds sprouting. **Cremini** are similar to the white button but are brown and have a somewhat meatier flavor. **Shiitakes** look almost like a parasol; quickly sauté in a nonstick pan and serve as a first course or side dish. **Portobellos** are large-capped and meaty—yummy grilled or broiled and served like little steaks. Or slice thickly and use in a pasta sauce. **Oyster mushrooms** are fan-shaped and are delicious in sautés and stews. **Porcini** are shaped like the white button but are much more flavorful. **Enoki** are long-stemmed with tiny little caps and can be served raw in salads or very quickly cooked in stir-fries or added to clear soups.

To Clean Mushrooms: Never soak mushrooms—this is not dunking-for-apples time. Mushrooms are like little sponges. Rinse them quickly or use a wet paper towel to rub clean. No reason to buy a little mushroom brush—a soft toothbrush will accomplish the same results.

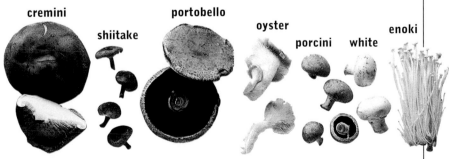

cremini
shiitake
portobello
oyster
porcini white
enoki

ayou Blackened Catfish

MAKES 4 SERVINGS

Prep: 10 minutes
Cook: 14 minutes

We never ate catfish when I was a child; it was one of those throw-away fish, a scavenger fish that fed off river bottoms. But now, it's everywhere! Most catfish you get in the supermarket is freshwater, and most of that is farm-raised, fed on a delicious diet of grains. Want to meet a lot of classy catfish in one place? Check out the World Catfish Festival every April in Belzoni, Mississippi. About 22,000 acres of ponds produce millions of pounds of fish. The trick for this dish is to make sure the skillet is very, very hot. Open the windows and have the fan going, or you'll be up on a step stool disconnecting the smoke alarm.

YOGURT–GREEN ONION SAUCE
$\frac{1}{2}$ cup nonfat plain yogurt
2 tablespoons finely chopped green onion (green and white parts)
$\frac{1}{8}$ teaspoon salt

1 pound catfish fillets, about $\frac{3}{4}$ inch thick
2 tablespoons Cajun spice mix
1 teaspoon vegetable oil
Lemon wedges, for garnish

1 Sauce: In small bowl combine yogurt, green onion, and salt. Refrigerate sauce, covered.

2 Heat cast-iron skillet or other heavy skillet over medium heat until very hot, 3 to 5 minutes.

3 Coat fish fillets on both sides with spice mix.

4 Add oil to skillet and heat. Add fish. Cook 2 to 4 minutes on each side or until opaque in center. Divide fish into four portions. Serve with sauce. Garnish with lemon.

Go-Withs

This is another one of those dishes where the percentage of calories from fat is high because this is a low-calorie dish. In addition, the actual grams of fat are only 10. Serve with corn on the cob and broiled tomato halves, and the percentage of fat for the whole meal will drop to 28%.

NUTRIENT VALUE PER SERVING
181 calories   18 g protein
10 g fat (50% fat)   4 g carbohydrate
406 mg sodium   52 mg cholesterol

Cajun Spice Mix

You can buy the already prepared spice mix, but if you have the time, it's fun to make your own. Try this one: 2 tablespoons paprika, 2 teaspoons chili powder, 1 teaspoon onion powder, 1 teaspoon dried oregano, 1 teaspoon dried marjoram, ¾ teaspoon salt, ½ teaspoon ground cumin, ¼ teaspoon ground cinnamon, and ¼ teaspoon cayenne pepper. This can be stored in a tightly capped jar in a cool dark place for up to a couple of weeks.

South Beach Halibut with Jade Sauce

MAKES 4 SERVINGS

Prep: 20 minutes
Cook: 7 to 10 minutes

I could have painted this picture in art school—isn't it a masterpiece! There is a very important lesson here. Food should always look beautiful. We first eat with our eyes, then our nose, and finally the taste buds get a chance. This is probably the "trendiest" recipe in the book, but it's good, and easy to make, since the salsa and the sauce can be made ahead. My inspiration for this recipe? A wonderful fish restaurant in South Beach, Florida, which will remain nameless, because it's already too popular and trendy.

NUTRIENT VALUE PER SERVING
216 calories   26 g protein
3 g fat (12% fat)   21 g carbohydrate
381 mg sodium   33 mg cholesterol

TROPICAL SALSA

- 1 ripe kiwifruit, peeled
- ½ ripe papaya, pitted and peeled
- ½ cup finely diced peeled cucumber
- ¼ cup finely diced red onion
- 1 tablespoon minced fresh cilantro
- 1 tablespoon rice wine vinegar
- ¼ teaspoon salt
- ⅛ to ¼ teaspoon red pepper flakes

HALIBUT

- ½ cup fat-free reduced-sodium chicken broth
- 1 pound fresh halibut *or* other firm-fleshed white fish, cut into serving size pieces

JADE SAUCE

- 5 ounces fresh spinach, stemmed, washed, and dried
- ½ cup *each* chopped green onion (green and white parts) *and* fresh cilantro *and* fresh basil
- 1 teaspoon minced peeled fresh ginger
- 1 tablespoon cornstarch
- ⅓ cup fat-free reduced-sodium chicken broth
- ¾ cup fat-free sour cream

1 Salsa: Finely dice kiwifruit and papaya. Combine in medium bowl with cucumber, onion, cilantro, vinegar, salt, and pepper flakes. Toss all together. Set aside.

2 Halibut: In medium skillet bring chicken broth to boil over medium heat. Add halibut. Lower heat. Cover. Gently simmer, 5 to 10 minutes or until fish is opaque

in center. With slotted spatula or spoon, remove fish from poaching liquid.

3 Jade Sauce: In blender or food processor puree spinach, green onion, cilantro, basil, and ginger.

4 In small saucepan dissolve cornstarch in chicken broth. Cook, stirring, over medium heat until mixture thickens, about 2 minutes. Add, together with sour cream to vegetables in blender or processor. Process until blended. Just before serving gently reheat in saucepan. Do not let boil. (Refrigerate the extra cup of sauce, covered, for up to 2 days for other uses.)

5 To serve: Spoon a pool of sauce, about ¼ cup, onto each of 4 dinner plates. Place fish on top. Spoon salsa over top.

Papaya and Fuzzy Fruit

Papaya, a semitropical fruit, is golden yellow on both the outside and inside and has a delectably sweet flesh. Although the black seeds are usually discarded, they are edible and delicious in salad dressings. A ripe papaya should yield slightly when gently squeezed — note the word "gently." Ripe fruit should be kept refrigerated; but if not ripe, it will ripen quickly at room temperature, especially in a brown-paper bag.

Fuzzy is probably the best way to describe a kiwifruit. Its interior, as you can see, is a brilliant green with tiny black edible seeds. The flavor? Sweet-tart, somewhere between strawberry and pineapple. Peel, slice, and use in desserts, salads, or as garnish. Refrigerate up to 3 weeks.

Cajun Gumbo

Prep: 15 minutes
Cook: 30 minutes

This is one of those dishes you cook by feel, and taste. Traditionally it can include chicken, sausage, ham, shrimp, crab, and oysters. But if you've got good leftovers in your refrigerator—vegetables, cooked meat, whatever—toss those in, too. Gumbo often takes hours, even days to prepare. The secret is in the roux—slowly cooking flour in fat until it's dark brown. It's good, let me tell you, but there's lots of fat. My version is streamlined, with little fat, and it's on the table in less than an hour. No waiting around.

1 Italian-style turkey sausage
1 cup boiling water
Nonstick olive oil cooking spray
1 cup sliced onion
½ cup *each* sliced green *and* red bell peppers
2 cloves garlic, finely chopped
2 cans (14½ ounces *each*) fat-free reduced-sodium chicken broth
4 ounces boneless, skinned chicken breast, cubed
⅓ cup all-purpose flour
½ teaspoon salt
¼ teaspoon freshly ground black pepper
⅛ to ¼ teaspoon cayenne pepper
4 ounces firm-fleshed fish, such as halibut, sea bass, *or* orange roughy, cubed
4 ounces cooked shelled medium shrimp
½ cup frozen okra, thawed (optional)
4 cups hot cooked white rice

1 Prick sausage with fork. In small saucepan of boiling water poach sausage 5 minutes to release excess fat. Drain.

2 Coat nonstick Dutch oven or large saucepan with cooking spray. Heat over medium-high heat. Add onion, green and red peppers, and garlic. Cook, stirring, 5 minutes, adding a little chicken broth as needed to prevent sticking and overbrowning.

3 Slice sausage into ½-inch-thick rounds. Add with cubed chicken to saucepan. Cook, stirring constantly, over medium-high heat 2 to 4 minutes or until browned, again adding a little chicken broth if needed to prevent sticking or overbrowning.

NUTRIENT VALUE PER SERVING
435 calories   25 g protein
4 g fat (8% fat)   71 g carbohydrate
951 mg sodium   71 mg cholesterol

4 In screw-top jar combine flour with
½ cup chicken broth. Cover tightly and
shake to mix to smooth paste. Stir into
saucepan. Cook over medium-high
heat, stirring constantly, until gravy is
browned and thickened, 3 to 4 minutes.

5 Add remaining chicken broth and
seasonings. Cook, whisking
occasionally, about 5 minutes.

6 Add fish. Cook 3 minutes. Add shrimp,
reserving 4 for garnish, and add okra if
using. Cook just to heat through, about
1 minute.

7 To serve: Coat four 1-cup custard cups
with cooking spray. Pack 1 cup rice into
each cup. Unmold in center of each
serving bowl. Spoon gumbo around
rice, and place a shrimp on top of rice.

Gumbo

The word "gumbo" itself comes from an African word
meaning okra. So there's a clue to how gumbo got to New
Orleans. In some gumbos okra is used as a thickener. The
trick is to not cook the gumbo much longer after the okra
has been added, or you'll get an icky texture.

*B*everly Hills Lasagna Rolls Royce

*W*e all know how to make lasagna with all that layering in a pan—but it takes forever. So here is my version, which is easier— and this is about as complicated as my recipes get. Not bad! What's nice about this dish is that everyone gets their very own lasagna rollup. Perfect for entertaining. And there's more good news. I use lots of vegetables, California style, with lots of seasonings—and no meat.

1 package (10 ounces) frozen chopped spinach, thawed
1 cup low-fat ricotta cheese
1 large egg white
½ teaspoon *each* dried basil *and* dried oregano
¼ teaspoon *each* garlic herb seasoning *and* ground nutmeg *and* salt
⅛ teaspoon freshly ground black pepper
¼ cup *each* shredded mozzarella cheese *and* grated Parmesan cheese
6 lasagna noodles, cooked *al dente* according to package directions and drained
1 can (14½ ounces) pasta-ready tomatoes with Italian seasoning

1 Preheat oven to 350°. Squeeze out all moisture from thawed spinach. Place in food processor. Add ricotta, egg white, basil, oregano, garlic seasoning, nutmeg, salt, pepper, half the mozzarella, and half the Parmesan cheese. Process until mixture is smooth and creamy.

2 To assemble rolls: Lay each cooked lasagna noodle on strip of wax paper. Dividing equally, spread spinach filling down length of each noodle. Roll up each noodle, jelly-roll style.

3 Spread one-third of tomatoes over bottom of shallow rectangular baking dish. Place each lasagna roll, seam side down, in dish. Spoon remaining tomatoes over rolls. Tent dish with aluminum foil.

NUTRIENT VALUE PER SERVING
206 calories   13 g protein
7 g fat (30% fat)   24 g carbohydrate
572 mg sodium   18 mg cholesterol

Say Cheese— But Carefully

Full-flavored cheeses taste great, but watch out—there's usually a lot of fat. The trick is to mix in a little low-fat cheese to keep the fat at bay but keep the rich taste. Hard cheeses with lots of flavor, such as Parmesan, are generally lower in fat, so you can use them a little more generously. In my lasagna I turn to low-fat ricotta, and you could use a part-skim milk mozzarella for even more fat savings. More about that ricotta. There are several kinds: whole milk, part-skim milk, low-fat (which we use in this recipe), and fat-free or nonfat. After tasting them all, we like the low-fat (and of course, we've always liked the whole milk and the part-skim)—but we're not really thrilled with the fat-free. But you be the judge—invite some friends over and try your own taste test.

4 Bake 35 minutes or until heated through. Remove foil. Sprinkle remaining mozzarella and Parmesan cheese over rolls. Bake, uncovered, 5 minutes more or until cheese has melted.

Note: For a colorful variation, cook ½ cup *each* diced red bell pepper *and* diced yellow summer squash in skillet coated with nonstick cooking spray until softened, about 4 minutes. Stir into spinach filling.

Easy Substitutions

You don't always have to use *our* ingredients. This recipe is a good example. You can replace the frozen spinach with frozen kale, or even collards for a Southern touch. Grated Romano works instead of the Parmesan, and how about a flavored lasagna noodle: spinach or tomato!

Spaghetti with Heavenly Meatballs

MAKES 4 SERVINGS

Prep: 20 minutes
Cook: 40 minutes

I love a huge plate of spaghetti drenched in marinara sauce, and topped with a 1 pound meatball. It's a single serving, just for me! But wait—here comes the portion patrol. O.K., O.K. In this recipe I use 6 ounces of pasta for 4 servings, and I make my 1-inch meatballs with ground turkey. I prepare my marinara sauce ahead, all 2 quarts. Turn this into a Saturday morning project, rather than watching cartoons and munching on a bag of jelly beans.

MARINARA SAUCE

- 1 cup chopped onion
- 1 can (14½ ounces) fat-free reduced-sodium chicken broth
- 2 teaspoons minced garlic
- 1 teaspoon *each* paprika *and* dried basil
- ½ teaspoon *each* salt *and* dried oregano
- ⅛ teaspoon *each* freshly ground black pepper *and* fennel seeds, crushed
- 1 can (28 ounces) crushed tomatoes in puree
- 1 can (28 ounces) whole tomatoes, undrained
- 2 teaspoons Worcestershire sauce
- ¼ cup chopped fresh parsley
- ½ teaspoon sugar, or to taste (optional)

TURKEY MEATBALLS

- 1 pound lean ground turkey
- ½ cup fresh bread crumbs
- ¼ cup finely chopped onion
- ¼ cup grated Parmesan cheese
- 2 tablespoons chopped fresh parsley
- 2 teaspoons minced garlic
- 2 large egg whites, beaten until frothy
- ½ teaspoon *each* salt *and* dried oregano *and* dried basil
- ¼ teaspoon freshly ground black pepper

Nonstick olive oil cooking spray

- 6 ounces uncooked spaghetti
- 2 cups Marinara Sauce *or* reduced-fat pasta-ready sauce
- ¼ cup grated Parmesan cheese

NUTRIENT VALUE PER SERVING
484 calories 37 g protein
16 g fat (30% fat) 47 g carbohydrate
662 mg sodium 92 mg cholesterol

NUTRIENT VALUE PER ½ CUP SAUCE
30 calories 1 g protein
trace of fat (11% fat) 6 g carbohydrate
371 mg sodium 0 mg cholesterol

1 Marinara Sauce: In large saucepan combine onion, chicken broth, garlic, paprika, basil, salt, oregano, pepper, and fennel seeds. Cook over medium heat 10 minutes or until broth is reduced by half.

2 Add crushed tomatoes and whole tomatoes with their liquid, Worcestershire sauce and parsley. Simmer, partially covered, over low heat for 30 minutes or until thickened and chunky. Add sugar to taste.

3 Turkey Meatballs: In large bowl combine turkey, bread crumbs, onion, Parmesan, parsley, garlic, beaten egg whites, salt, oregano, basil, and pepper. Mix lightly but thoroughly.

4 With moistened hands, lightly shape mixture into 1-inch balls. You should have about 36. Coat large nonstick skillet with cooking spray. Heat over medium-high heat. Add meatballs, about 8 at a time. Cook, stirring constantly, until browned, about 2 to 3 minutes per batch. Re-coat skillet with cooking spray as needed. When all meatballs are browned, return them to skillet. Over medium heat, continue to cook, shaking skillet to turn meatballs, about 5 minutes or until cooked through.

5 Meanwhile, cook spaghetti in large pot of boiling salted water. Drain. In medium saucepan, heat sauce.

6 Divide hot pasta and meatballs onto 4 serving plates. Ladle ½ cup sauce over each plate. Sprinkle with ¼ cup Parmesan, dividing equally.

Note: Divide and freeze remaining Marinara Sauce into 1-cup portions. For a smoother consistency, puree in a blender or food processor.

Heavenly Meatballs

My mother Shirley's secret for light meatballs is to handle them gently and lovingly, like little clouds. Mush the meat too much, and you'll have very dense, compact nuggets—perfect for playing marbles.

Sheboygan Three-Cheese Macaroni

MAKES 6 SERVINGS

Prep: 10 minutes
Cook: 10 minutes
Bake: 350° for 20 minutes

This is it—the American classic from Sheboygan, Wisconsin, the heart of Wisconsin dairyland. And if you think macaroni and cheese only comes in a blue box—wrong! You can actually make it yourself, from scratch, without all those preservatives and heavy, goppy cheeses. My secret? You have to read the recipe. I even manage to sneak in a slice of crispy bacon (Sacred Fat). When Thomas Jefferson served macaroni and cheese at a White House dinner, one guest found it disagreeable. If mine had been served, I'm sure the guest would have run straight to the kitchen for the recipe, Secret Service or no Secret Service.

NUTRIENT VALUE PER SERVING
297 calories   23 g protein
7 g fat (21% fat)   36 g carbohydrate
709 mg sodium   21 mg cholesterol

2 cups elbow macaroni
½ cup chopped onion
2 tablespoons chopped sun-dried
tomatoes (not packed in oil)
6 cups boiling water
1½ cups low-fat cottage cheese
1 tablespoon Dijon-style mustard
½ cup evaporated skim milk
¼ teaspoon *each* salt *and* freshly ground
black pepper
1 tablespoon chopped fresh basil
or 1 teaspoon dried basil
¼ cup chopped fresh parsley
1 cup shredded reduced-fat cheddar
cheese
4 tablespoons grated Parmesan cheese
Nonstick vegetable oil cooking spray
1 slice bacon, cooked crisp and crumbled
1 slice whole-wheat bread, finely crumbed
6 cherry tomatoes, sliced into rounds

1 Preheat oven to 350°. In large saucepan
cook macaroni, onion, and sun-dried
tomatoes in boiling water until just
tender.

2 While macaroni is cooking, combine
cottage cheese, mustard, and milk in
blender or food processor. Season with
salt and pepper. Blend until smooth.

3 Drain cooked macaroni mixture in
colander. Place in large bowl. Sprinkle
with basil and parsley.

4 Stir in cottage cheese mixture. Fold in
cheddar and 3 tablespoons Parmesan
cheese. Mix thoroughly.

5 Coat shallow 2-quart casserole with
nonstick spray. Spoon in macaroni
mixture.

6 In small bowl mix remaining
1 tablespoon Parmesan with crumbled
bacon and bread crumbs. Sprinkle over
macaroni. Arrange cherry tomato slices
in 3 rows over top.

7 Bake 20 minutes or until top is lightly
golden and macaroni is bubbly. Garnish
with parsley sprigs, if desired.

Reduced-Fat Cheeses

Sometime when you're making a supermarket run, plan to
spend a little time checking out the cheese section. Many
supermarkets now have two spots for cheese—the usual
refrigerator section in the dairy department, and a
freestanding case with specialty cheeses. If you have
paper and pencil for note taking, even better. Read labels
and look at the difference between lite, reduced-fat, no-
fat, part-skim, and all the other variations. Keep an eye
out for reduced-sodium, too. Remember, the supermarket
is always the best place to do your research—but never do
it on an empty stomach. Here's a list of reduced-fat
cheeses to check out: cheddar, Colby, Monterey Jack,
Muenster, provolone, part-skim mozzarella, Gouda,
Edam, Swiss (Jarlsberg), cream cheese (Neufchâtel),
cottage cheese, and part-skim ricotta.

All About Eve Pasta

Prep: 15 minutes
Cook: 15 minutes

Yes, this spaghetti dish, with all its seductive vegetables from the Garden of Eden, will soon become your best friend. One of the real pleasures here—and without sin—is the Yogurt Cheese: creamy and flirtatious, but practically without fat.

Asparagus on Parade

Want to see 12,000 acres of asparagus? Well, trek off to the towns of Shelby and Hart, Michigan, for the National Asparagus Festival. You won't believe the food—everything including meatballs in a sweet-and-sour asparagus sauce, asparagus cakes, and lime jello with shredded asparagus. Can you imagine?

NUTRIENT VALUE PER SERVING
329 calories   15 g protein
3 g fat (10% fat)   59 g carbohydrate
532 mg sodium   6 mg cholesterol

Nonstick olive oil cooking spray
2 tablespoons chopped shallots
1 clove garlic, chopped
1 cup quartered button mushrooms
½ cup fat-free reduced-sodium chicken broth
½ cup sliced carrot
1 cup diagonally sliced sugar snap peas
½ cup sliced fresh asparagus
½ cup nonfat plain Yogurt Cheese (see opposite page)
2 tablespoons thinly sliced fresh basil
4 medium plum tomatoes, peeled, seeded, and cut up
¼ teaspoon salt
Freshly ground black pepper, to taste
8 ounces thin spaghetti, cooked according to package directions and drained
¼ cup grated Parmesan cheese
4 sprigs fresh basil, for garnish

1 Coat nonstick saucepan with cooking spray. Heat over medium-high heat. Add shallots, garlic, and mushrooms. Cook, stirring, adding splashes of chicken broth as needed to prevent overbrowning, until softened, about 3 minutes. Add remaining chicken broth and carrot. Simmer 3 minutes.

2 Add snap peas and asparagus. Cook 3 minutes. Stir in Yogurt Cheese, basil, and tomatoes. (Make sure sauce doesn't boil after Yogurt Cheese is added, or sauce may separate.) Season with salt and pepper to taste. Toss with pasta. Sprinkle with Parmesan. Garnish with basil.

Yogurt Cheese

The secret to the low-fat creamy pasta sauce is yogurt cheese that you make yourself. It's easy. Just spoon plain nonfat yogurt (without added gelatin) into a sieve or strainer lined with a double thickness of cheesecloth or a paper coffee filter, set over a bowl or measuring cup, and place in the refrigerator. All the excess liquid will drain out of the yogurt, and the longer you let the yogurt sit, the denser the cheese will be. Let it drain overnight, and the amount of yogurt will reduce almost by half. This cheese is good for lots of other things, too: in any sauce where you would use heavy cream (just don't let it boil), or flavored with fruit purees for a dessert topping.

SIDE BY SIDE

BY SIDE

Corny-as-Kansas-in-August Corn Pudding

MAKES 4 SERVINGS

Prep: 15 minutes
Cook: 8 minutes
Bake: 350° for 55 to 60 minutes

This recipe title is a mouthful, and so is this delicious pudding. Just whisper "pudding" in my ear, and I'll smile every time. And thank you, Kansas, for all that corn.

Low-Fat Tricks

Evaporated skim milk thickened with a little flour fools you into thinking you're eating fat—but trust me, you're not. Evaporated milk is fresh whole milk with about 60 percent of the water removed, and vitamin D added. Although it comes in a whole-milk version, you want the skim, which has one-half percent butterfat or less. Liquid egg replacement is the other fat-fooling trick I often use. Check the label to make sure you're using one you can bake with.

Nonstick butter-flavored cooking spray
$\frac{1}{3}$ cup *each* finely chopped onion *and* red bell pepper
1 bag (16 ounces) frozen corn, thawed and drained
$\frac{1}{4}$ cup all-purpose flour
1 can (12 ounces) evaporated skim milk
$\frac{1}{2}$ cup liquid egg replacement
2 teaspoons sugar
2 teaspoons Dijon-style mustard
$\frac{1}{2}$ teaspoon *each* salt *and* baking powder
$\frac{1}{8}$ teaspoon cayenne

1 Preheat oven to 350°. Coat $1\frac{1}{2}$-quart casserole or soufflé dish with cooking spray.

2 Coat medium nonstick skillet with cooking spray. Heat over medium heat. Add onion and red pepper. Cook, stirring, 5 minutes or until softened. Add corn. Cook, stirring, 3 more minutes. Remove from heat.

3 In large bowl whisk together flour and $\frac{1}{2}$ cup milk. Mix in remaining milk and all remaining ingredients, including cooked corn mixture. Using rubber spatula, scrape corn pudding mixture into prepared casserole. Place casserole in shallow baking pan. Place in oven. Pour enough hot water into baking pan to come halfway up sides of casserole dish.

4 Bake 55 to 60 minutes or until set.

NUTRIENT VALUE PER SERVING
234 calories   15 g protein
1 g fat (3% fat)   45 g carbohydrate
542 mg sodium   3 mg cholesterol

Once-Is-Not-Enough Boise Baked Potatoes

MAKES 4 SERVINGS

Prep: 20 minutes
Bake: 400° for 1 hour 10 minutes

These potatoes are baked not just once, but twice. And they're stuffed. You may have noticed I love surprises in my food— something wonderful waiting inside. I use broccoli in this stuffing, but you could substitute cooked carrots, red and yellow bell peppers, green beans, and any other vegetable that is your favorite. Other reduced-fat cheeses would be delicious: Monterey Jack, Muenster, Swiss. This is a recipe you can re-invent.

Sacred Fat

One slice of bacon, cooked until crisp and then crumbled over each of four potatoes. Who would have thought you could do that and still keep it low-fat?

NUTRIENT VALUE PER SERVING
227 calories   11 g protein
2 g fat (8% fat)   45 g carbohydrate
286 mg sodium   6 mg cholesterol

2 large russet or baking potatoes, scrubbed

½ cup fat-free sour cream

¼ cup chopped green onion (green and white parts)

1 tablespoon reduced-sodium soy sauce

½ teaspoon freshly ground black pepper

1 package (10 ounces) frozen chopped broccoli, thawed, *or* 1⅓ cups lightly steamed fresh broccoli flowerets, chopped, *or* 1 cup ratatouille (see Carnival Confetti Potatoes, page 32)

¼ cup shredded reduced-fat cheddar cheese

1 slice bacon, cooked crisp and crumbled

1 Preheat oven to 400°. Bake potatoes on oven rack 1 hour or until soft. Holding potatoes with potholders, cut each potato in half lengthwise. Scoop out potato insides, leaving about ¼-inch-thick layer of potato inside skin; place potato insides in medium bowl.

2 Mash sour cream, green onion, soy sauce, and pepper into potato in bowl.

3 If using frozen broccoli, drain and squeeze out excess moisture. Mix broccoli or ratatouille into potato mixture. Divide filling into 4 potato halves. Top with cheese. Sprinkle with bacon. Place on baking sheet.

4 Bake 10 minutes or until heated through and cheese has melted.

Potatoes Are Forever!

No more the day of just plain potatoes—now they come plain and fancy. And leave those skins on, since nutritionally most of the fiber, iron, and other minerals are in or close to the skin. **All-purpose potatoes,** with their thin, light brown skin, are just that— all-purpose. Cut them up and boil, steam, pan-fry, or roast. **Russets** (these include Idaho) are long, with a coarse, dark skin. Cooked, their flesh becomes fluffy, perfect for baked potatoes or French fries—ooops, I mean oven fries. And then there is the **small round potato,** red or white; small **Peruvian Blue,** with its fabulous indigo color and very potato-y taste; and **Yukon Gold** and **Finnish Butter**, both golden-colored and so richly flavored they need no added fat, such as butter (perish the thought!)

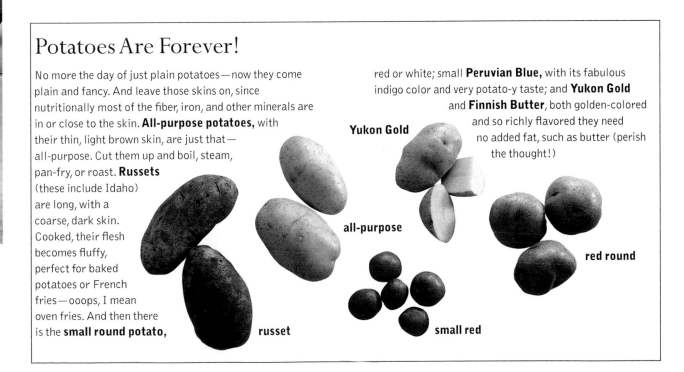

Yukon Gold

all-purpose

russet

small red

red round

It's-Not-Dessert Scalloped Sweet Potatoes

MAKES 4 SERVINGS

Prep: 15 minutes
Bake: 425° for 1 hour 15 minutes

Like the T.V. commercial says, there are some things that are too important to share, such as seat belts. When I first started putting this cookbook together, I said no way was I going to include this recipe (which really can't make up its mind whether it's a dessert or a vegetable side dish). After many sleepless nights (some in Seattle) and feeling guilty about being selfish, I decided to share it with you. But it comes with a warning—it's so good, you really just have to cut one piece and then run into another room to eat it, because once you start, you'll want to eat the whole thing.

1 (9-inch) ready-prepared reduced-fat graham cracker crust
2 cups peeled, thinly sliced sweet potatoes or yams
1 navel orange, peeled, sliced into thin rounds, then cut into small pieces
1 tablespoon (packed) golden brown sugar
⅓ cup fresh orange juice
¼ teaspoon pumpkin pie spice
Pinch *each* ground cinnamon *and* ground nutmeg
1 tablespoon maple syrup
1 tablespoon light butter

1 Preheat oven to 425°. Cover bottom of pie crust with single overlapping layer of potatoes. Top with layer of orange pieces. Repeat layers, ending with potatoes.

2 In small bowl stir sugar into orange juice. Pour over top of potatoes. Sprinkle with spices. Cover.

3 Bake 1 hour. Uncover. Drizzle maple syrup over top. Dot with butter. Bake 15 minutes more or until top is golden brown and potatoes are tender.

NUTRIENT VALUE PER SERVING
375 calories   4 g protein
9 g fat (21% fat)   68 g carbohydrate
231 mg sodium   0 mg cholesterol

A Yam, by Any Other Name,
Is a Sweet Potato

yam

sweet potato

What's called a yam in this country is usually a sweet potato.
Popular in Latin American countries, yams are seldom grown in this
country. The two tubers are actually from different plant species.
The **yam** has brown skin and yellow or white flesh and contains more natural
sugar and moisture. The **sweet potato** with its dark orange skin and orange
flesh is a better source of vitamins A and C. Here's a tip: The darker the color
of the skin, the sweeter and more flavorful the sweet potato.

Salinas Two-Toned Broccoli

MAKES 4 SERVINGS

Prep: 15 minutes
Cook: 5 minutes

1 bunch broccoli
Garlic-flavored olive oil (see Garlic-Oil Mist)
2 tablespoons shaved Parmesan cheese
1 tablespoon fresh lemon juice (optional)

No, Salinas was not our French Quarter cook who loved to deep-fry broccoli. Salinas Valley, California—that's where 90 percent of all our broccoli is grown. There's something magical in California sunshine.

1 Cut off thick broccoli stems. Peel stems. Cut stems crosswise into rounds or buttons, ⅛ inch thick. Peel small stems attached to flowerets. Place stem slices and flowerets in steamer basket. Steam over boiling water in covered saucepan for 5 minutes or until tender.

2 Arrange broccoli "coins" on serving plate or dinner plates, with flowerets in center. Lightly spritz with oil. Top with Parmesan curls. Sprinkle with lemon juice if using, just before serving. (Lemon discolors broccoli, so don't add until the last moment.)

Close Shave

Slide a swivel-bladed vegetable peeler along a block of Parmesan cheese to create beautiful, almost petal-like shavings. They're excellent in this dish as well as over other vegetables, pasta, potatoes, and on and on.

Garlic-Oil Mist

You've heard of gorillas in the mist—well, this is broccoli in the mist. Buy a little plastic pump spray and fill it with a good-quality olive oil, preferably extra-virgin, and one or two cloves of crushed garlic. Refrigerate for up to about 2 weeks. To use, place the bottle under running hot water to desolidify the oil, which will harden up from being refrigerated. Spray on cooked vegetables, over a potato, or on chicken before cooking—you get the idea.

NUTRIENT VALUE PER SERVING
43 calories   4 g protein
1 g fat (20% fat)   5 g carbohydrate
82 mg sodium   2 mg cholesterol

The Nutritional Darling of the Vegetable Set

In 1992 it was reported that broccoli (along with other cruciferous vegetables, those with cross-shaped flower petals) may play an important role in helping to reduce certain kinds of cancer. Shopping carts in supermarket checkout lines were piled high with broccoli and garden shops couldn't keep up with the demand for broccoli seeds. But some of us always knew that broccoli was good for you, even if President Bush didn't like the cute little fellow—an excellent source of calcium, and goodly amounts of vitamins A and C and some Bs, as well as potassium and iron, and all-important fiber.

Broccoli, Banquet Style
Although ancient Rome collapsed with all that fast living, Romans did eat their broccoli as part of the vegetable course at their banquets.

Save the Stalks
I'm going to start an environmental movement to "Save the Stalks." Drive across America and you'll see the highways littered with little broccoli stalks, trying to take root. I love this recipe because it uses that ugly part of the vegetable that most people throw out. Not me. For this dish, I peel the stalks and then slice them into beautiful "coins." I arrange them on a platter, and then I make a gorgeous broccoli floweret forest grow in the center.

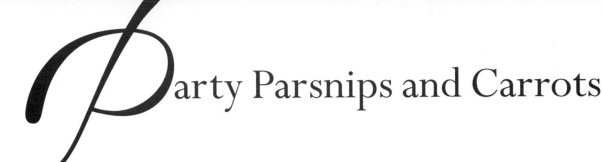

Party Parsnips and Carrots

MAKES 6 SERVINGS

Prep: 20 minutes
Bake: 400° for 1 to 1½ hours

From a distance these look like French fries—how did they sneak into this book! But wait a second. They're the most delicious roasted vegetables you've ever had. The natural sweetness of the parsnips and carrots gets even better as the vegetables slowly caramelize in the oven. You have to eat them exactly my way. Put two carrot sticks and two parsnip sticks in your mouth all at once. You won't believe the combination of flavors. And you'll never think about parsnips the same way again.

1 pound *each* carrots *and* parsnips, peeled and cut into 3 x ¼ x ¼-inch sticks
1 teaspoon olive oil

1 Preheat oven to 400°. Spread vegetable sticks in single layer on nonstick baking sheet. Sprinkle vegetables with olive oil. Toss until well coated.

2 Bake, tossing vegetables frequently, 1 to 1½ hours or until crisp and golden.

A Tisket, A Tasket

These potato baskets filled with vegetables are so pretty you can use them for decorations around the house. Try other fillings in the baskets: peas, chopped green beans, even small broccoli flowerets. To make the baskets, partially cook 3 large russet potatoes in a microwave oven (see manufacturer's instructions) on HIGH power for 12 minutes, or bake at 400° for 45 minutes, until nearly tender. Halve crosswise. Hollow out insides, leaving ½-inch-thick shell. Trim the rounded ends so potato halves will stand up. Coat nonstick baking sheet with cooking spray. Place potato halves, rim side down, on baking sheet. Bake at 400° for 30 minutes or until skins are crisp, rims are golden brown, and potatoes are tender. Stand the potatoes up and fill them with the roasted parsnips and carrots.

Makes 6 potato bowls for holding vegetable filling.

Give Parsnips a Chance

And on the eighth day God created the parsnip—He almost forgot it! Thank goodness he didn't. Because they really are delicious and very sweet tasting. Part of the parsnip problem may be a case of mistaken identity. Do you know a parsnip when you see one? Don't confuse it with a daikon, that long white radish, which can be pretty bitter. Read the produce signs carefully, or ask your produce person. Use parsnips anywhere you would use cooked carrots.

NUTRIENT VALUE PER SERVING
102 calories   2 g protein
1 g fat (8% fat)   23 g carbohydrate
54 mg sodium   0 mg cholesterol

Woodstock Wild Rice

Y ou have to wear a plaid shirt and hiking boots when you make this. No ifs, ands, or buts. This is real he-man stuff, full of mushrooms, chopped onion, and a little lemon zest for zip. If you've never cooked with some of the specialty mushrooms now available in the supermarket, try them here (see page 131). They'll be perfect with the strong nutty flavor of the wild rice.

1 can (14½ ounces) fat-free reduced-sodium chicken broth
1 cup water
½ cup wild rice
½ cup white rice
1½ cups sliced fresh mushrooms
1 clove garlic, minced
½ teaspoon salt
Pinch of saffron *or* turmeric
½ cup chopped green onion (green and white parts)
¼ cup chopped fresh parsley
2 teaspoons grated lemon zest
Strips of lemon zest *and* sprigs of flat-leaf Italian parsley

1 In medium saucepan bring chicken broth and water to boil over medium heat. Add wild rice. Simmer, covered, over low heat for 25 minutes.

2 Uncover. Add white rice, mushrooms, garlic, salt, and saffron. Bring to boil again. Cover. Simmer 20 minutes or until rice is tender and most of liquid is absorbed.

3 Remove from heat. Stir in green onion and parsley. Cover and let stand 10 minutes. Just before serving, stir in lemon zest. Garnish with strips of lemon zest and sprigs of parsley.

Saffron—Even Pricier Than Wild Rice

This is the world's most expensive spice. It takes more than 200,000 stigmas (count them!) from a special crocus to make 1 pound of saffron. Saffron adds a beautiful yellow-orange color and a subtle flavor to dishes. Turmeric— much, much cheaper, and less flavorful—can be used as a substitute.

NUTRIENT VALUE PER SERVING
183 calories   6 g protein
1 g fat (3% fat)   39 g carbohydrate
559 mg sodium   0 mg cholesterol

The Rice That's Not a Rice

Wild rice is not a rice at all—it's really a grass. Native Americans in the lake region of Minnesota still harvest it in much the same way they always have. Since there is not a huge harvest every year of wild rice, the price tends to be higher than white. But because of its strong flavor, a little goes a long way, so it can be easily extended with white rice. You have to be patient when you cook this—it's not like quick rice.

Tranquillity Rice

Prep: 10 minutes
Cook: 50 minutes

I borrowed this recipe from the days when I was a vegetarian. During the Seventies I remember walking into vegetarian restaurants in L.A. Everyone spoke very quietly, eating their brown rice. My version is even more spiritual, since it contains Sacred Fat (the sesame seeds). Feeling apprehensive and agitated? One spoonful of this will give you that inner calm feeling.

Nonstick vegetable oil cooking spray
$\frac{1}{2}$ cup chopped onion
1 can (14$\frac{1}{2}$ ounces) fat-free reduced-sodium chicken broth
$\frac{1}{4}$ cup water
1 tablespoon dry sherry
1 tablespoon reduced-sodium soy sauce
1 teaspoon dark sesame oil
$\frac{1}{8}$ to $\frac{1}{4}$ teaspoon hot pepper sauce
1 cup uncooked brown rice
$\frac{1}{3}$ cup chopped green onion (green and white parts)
$\frac{1}{2}$ cup chopped drained canned water chestnuts
2 tablespoons sesame seeds, lightly toasted (see Note below)
Green onion strips, for garnish (optional)

1 Coat large nonstick skillet with cooking spray. Heat over high heat. Add onion. Cook, stirring constantly, 3 minutes or until lightly softened.

2 Add chicken broth, water, sherry, soy sauce, sesame oil, and hot sauce. Bring to boil. Stir in rice. Cover. Reduce heat. Simmer 45 minutes or until liquid is absorbed and rice is tender.

3 Remove from heat. Stir in green onion and water chestnuts. Before serving, sprinkle with sesame seeds. Garnish with green onion strips, if desired.

Note: To toast sesame seeds, heat in dry nonstick skillet over medium heat, stirring frequently, 2 to 3 minutes or until lightly browned and aromatic.

NUTRIENT VALUE PER SERVING
270 calories   7 g protein
6 g fat (22% fat)   44 g carbohydrate
418 mg sodium   0 mg cholesterol

Fargo Garlic Mashed Potatoes

MAKES 4 SERVINGS

Prep: 10 minutes
Cook: 20 minutes

Do you know why Fargo, North Dakota, is so sparsely populated? These potatoes were served in all the diners there, resulting in such a garlic-breath epidemic that everybody left town. I know, it's hard to believe. People will tell you that roasting or baking whole heads of garlic tames the flavor. Not true. It tames and sweetens it a little, but that smell clings to your taste buds like a Sophia Loren movie.

4 small russet or baking potatoes, peeled and halved
1 head Roasted Roses of Garlic (page 164), made into paste
¼ cup skim milk, warmed
2 tablespoons light butter
¼ teaspoon salt
Pinch of white pepper
Chopped fresh parsley, for garnish (optional)

1 In medium saucepan cover potatoes with about 2 inches water. Bring to boil. Reduce heat. Simmer, covered, about 10 minutes or until potatoes are tender. Drain, reserving ¼ cup of the potato water. Keep potatoes warm.

2 In medium bowl mash potatoes thoroughly with potato masher. Add roasted garlic paste, milk, butter, salt, and pepper. Beat with masher or wooden spoon until potatoes are light and fluffy. Add some or all reserved potato water as needed if potatoes seem dry. Garnish with parsley, if desired.

The Best Guarded Secret: Potato Water

Don't throw out that water you cook the potatoes in — never, never, never. It's better than Holy Water. Write the Vatican. It's what I stir into my mashed potatoes to make them fluffy, rather than heavy cream. And if there's any water left over, drizzle it over your plants and watch them grow.

NUTRIENT VALUE PER SERVING
174 calories   3 g protein
5 g fat (28% fat)   29 g carbohydrate
202 mg sodium   0 mg cholesterol

Mashed Potatoes to the Max

When I have a craving for the mashed, I show up at Drai's, a restaurant in L.A., and treat friends to their sampler plate: the most elegant miniature copper pans, full of flavored mashed potatoes. My current favorites? Onion, spinach, garlic, and the traditional plain. Rumor has it that another restaurant now offers citrus and pesto. Where will this spud-mania stop?

A Nutrition Gold Mine

This unassuming spud is practically ideal. Just a trace of fat, a little sodium, and (for a medium-size potato), about 220 calories. Now here's the punch line: an excellent source of vitamin C and B-6 and niacin, as well as fiber and potassium. I love them so much I call them spud-studs.

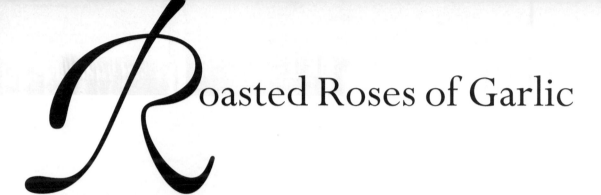

Roasted Roses of Garlic

Prep: 2 minutes
Bake: 375° for 1 hour

This is the best. It's one of those tasty tidbits I offer people when they drop by the house and start sniffing in the kitchen, opening cupboard doors, and peeking in the refrigerator. You can see it in their eyes. What's Richard going to surprise us with? Ta-da! I open the oven door and there they are: caramel-y, roasted small heads of garlic, what I call my "roses" of garlic—all glisten-y. I snip off the tops, and the garlic butter (no cholesterol and very little fat, thank you) just oozes out. Such a flurry! People can't wait to spread it on the thin pieces of toast I have in a basket on the counter. Got the picture?

1   whole head garlic
1   teaspoon olive oil

1   Preheat oven to 375°.

2   Place garlic on folded-over double layers of aluminum foil. Drizzle with olive oil. Seal foil.

3   Bake 1 hour. Unwrap and let cool. Cut across pointed end of garlic head. Squeeze out garlic paste into small bowl. Use as desired.

Garlic Madness

If you love garlic so much you could inhale it, then visit the annual garlic festival in Gilroy, California. When you're about 20 miles away, you'll know you're getting close—just stick your head out the car window and sniff the air. Some of the dishes you can sample?—the usual garlic soup, chicken with 40 cloves, and garlic mayonnaise. But how about garlic ice cream, garlic cheesecake, and a garlic chocolate mousse? Will Rogers described Gilroy as "the only town in America where you can marinate a steak by hanging it on a clothesline."

Simmons Roasted Garlic Potion

I personally like to use this as a face cream! Just kidding. But besides spreading this on toast or vegetables, I love to stir a spoonful into beef stews and soups, toss a dab with cooked pasta, and shake a thimbleful with salad dressings. It's outrageous!

NUTRIENT VALUE PER TEASPOON
21 calories   1 g protein
1 g fat (43% fat)   3 g carbohydrate
1 mg sodium   0 mg cholesterol

Cheesecake with a New York City Accent

Prep: 10 minutes
Bake: 325° for 45 minutes
Chill: 3 hours

When I was a kid, I had my first cheesecake at the Stage Delicatessen in New York City— a pivotal moment. I felt God must have made this especially for me. Well, that one slice wasn't enough. I ran next door to Wolf's deli to try their cheesecake. Then there was Lindy's. After that, off on a subway to Brooklyn to Junior's. I discovered all kinds. After years of tasting, my favorite was like a dessert Brie—almost runny in the center. My cheesecake here is best eaten chilled. But I must admit that I've snitched a piece while it's still warm, and gooey in the center.

3 packages (8 ounces *each*) fat-free cream cheese (not whipped)
¾ cup sugar
1½ teaspoons vanilla extract
¾ cup liquid egg substitute
½ teaspoon grated lemon zest
1½ teaspoons fresh lemon juice
Nonstick butter-flavored cooking spray
⅓ cup low-fat graham-cracker crumbs (about 4 whole crackers)
Mixed fresh berries, for garnish (optional)

1 Preheat oven to 325°. In large mixing bowl, using electric mixer, beat together cream cheese, sugar, and vanilla until well blended. Add egg substitute, lemon zest, and lemon juice. Beat just enough to blend, no more.

2 Coat base and sides of 8-inch springform pan or 9-inch pie plate with cooking spray. Add graham cracker crumbs and shake pan so crumbs cling to bottom and sides. Shake excess crumbs into small bowl. Pour cream cheese mixture into prepared pan. Dust top lightly with some of the remaining crumbs.

3 Bake 45 minutes or until center is almost set. (If done in pie plate, cake will rise and fall, with some cracking around outside edge—this is fine.) Transfer pan or plate to wire rack. Cool. Refrigerate at least 3 hours before serving. Garnish with mixed berries, if desired.

NUTRIENT VALUE PER SERVING
163 calories   13 g protein
1 g fat (6% fat)   24 g carbohydrate
388 mg sodium   5 mg cholesterol

Brownie Points

Prep: 15 minutes
Bake: 350° for 35 minutes

I always wanted to be a Brownie because they made s'mores and other good things. Cub Scouts just whittled and earned merit badges. But I must tell you that every year at Christmas time, on my birthday, and for other major occasions, people send me thousands of items of food. You'd think I'd get healthy things. Not a chance—it's grandmother's special fudgy brownie. One year I buried all this stuff in the backyard so I wouldn't be tempted. But at five o'clock in the morning, I was out there digging it up—culinary tales from the crypt.

NUTRIENT VALUE PER BROWNIE
118 calories   2 g protein
3 g fat (22% fat)   20 g carbohydrate
40 mg sodium   trace of cholesterol

Nonstick vegetable oil cooking spray

½ cup all-purpose flour

3 tablespoons unsweetened cocoa powder

¼ teaspoon baking powder

⅓ cup nonfat cream cheese, softened

1 cup sugar

3½ ounces semisweet chocolate, melted

5 teaspoons vegetable oil

¼ cup liquid egg substitute

2 teaspoons vanilla extract

1 cup fresh *or* frozen raspberries (optional)

1 Preheat oven to 350°. Coat 8 x 8 x 2-inch-square baking pan with cooking spray.

2 In medium bowl stir together flour, cocoa powder, and baking powder.

3 In second medium bowl, with electric mixer beat together cream cheese and sugar until creamy. Beat in melted chocolate and oil. Gradually beat in egg substitute and vanilla. On low speed, beat in flour mixture until smooth. Fold in raspberries if using. Spoon into prepared pan.

4 Bake for 35 minutes or until firm. Cool pan on wire rack. Cut into 16 pieces.

Low-Fat Tricks

We've come a long way since the brownies of the Fifties and Sixties. Those were loaded with fat, sometimes as much as 25 to 30 grams of fat—butter and eggs will do it every time. In my brownie, which is very fudgy, I use egg substitute and vegetable oil—no whole eggs or butter. The special trick is nonfat cream cheese, which adds the feel and richness of fat.

Cocoa Powder

This is great for making low-fat chocolate desserts, since most of the cocoa butter or fat has been removed. Keep in mind that Dutch-process cocoa powder contains more fat than regular unsweetened cocoa powder. And never, never substitute instant cocoa or other mixes, which contain sugar and other no-no's.

Brownie Variations on a Theme

I like fun shapes. Food should be fun. So I often cut brownies into diamonds, hearts, or stars, and then dust them with cocoa powder and/or confectioners' sugar. Fat-free fudge sauce drizzled over the top is not a bad addition, or a dollop of reduced-fat sour cream or nonfat frozen yogurt. In fact, you can sandwich two brownies together, s'more style, with the frozen yogurt.

Gift-Wrapped Apple Pie

MAKES 12 SERVINGS

Prep: 30 minutes
Bake: 350° for 1 hour 15 minutes

Everybody has his or her own version of apple pie, but this is really spectacular. The phyllo crust is all crunchy and crumbly. I remember when I was little, standing in the gift-wrapping line at holiday time. If I wanted a bigger bow or the more expensive wrapping paper, I would bat my eyes. For this beautifully wrapped pie, you don't have to flirt, since it already comes with its own phyllo pastry gift paper.

2 heaping tablespoons raisins
¼ cup orange juice
6 cups sliced peeled green apples, such as Pippin or Granny Smith
2 tablespoons fresh lemon juice
¼ cup (packed) light brown sugar
2 tablespoons all-purpose flour
½ teaspoon ground cinnamon
Pinch of ground cloves
6 sheets phyllo dough, thawed according to package directions
Nonstick butter-flavored cooking spray
⅓ cup finely ground low-fat graham-cracker crumbs (about 4 whole crackers)
2 tablespoons sugar-free apricot fruit spread, warmed

1 In small bowl soak raisins in orange juice. In large bowl toss apples with lemon juice. In second small bowl mix together sugar, flour, cinnamon, and cloves. Sprinkle over apples. Toss to mix.

2 Preheat oven to 350°. Lay damp clean dish towel on counter; cover with wax paper. Lay phyllo dough sheets on top of wax paper. Then fold towel, wax paper, and phyllo sheets in half like a book. As if reading a book, open "cover" (towel) and "inside cover" (wax paper) Open first "page" of phyllo; coat with cooking spray. Then sprinkle lightly with cracker crumbs. Continue in same manner to middle of "book," coating each "page" with cooking spray, followed by light sprinkling of cracker crumbs. Close "book." Then starting this time from "back cover," repeat previous coating and

NUTRIENT VALUE PER SERVING
108 calories   1 g protein
1 g fat (9% fat)   24 g carbohydrate
69 mg sodium   0 mg cholesterol

sprinkling, working toward middle of "book." It is important to work quickly to prevent phyllo from drying out.

3 Coat 10-inch pie plate with cooking spray. Lift 3 phyllo sheets together and lay them across and into pie plate. Lift remaining 3 sheets and lay them at right angles to first 3 sheets. Let them fold and crinkle. Gently ease sheets down into pan, leaving excess hanging over edge.

4 Brush bottom of pie shell with warmed apricot fruit spread. Drain raisins, discarding orange juice. Mix raisins with apples. Pour apple mixture into pie plate. Gently bring up phyllo to cover apples. Center of pie will be open.

5 Bake 1 hour to 1 hour 15 minutes, until apples feel soft when tested with wooden pick and phyllo is golden brown. If phyllo begins to brown too much, tent lightly with aluminum foil.

Phyllo Pastry

When Greeks immigrated to this country, they brought with them their phyllo pastry, the Mediterranean version of strudel. The word *phyllo* in Greek means leaves. The most famous phyllo dessert as you know is baklava. You can buy phyllo pastry in your supermarket, in the freezer or refrigerator sections, or if you're lucky enough, you may even find it fresh in a Greek grocery store. It comes in a long rectangular package, with all the tissue-thin leaves of pastry dough layered on top of each other like a book, folded over in a neat package. Contrary to what most people think, it does not come with a quarter pound of butter smeared between each layer, nor do you need to buy 3 pounds of the fat. In this recipe I show you how to layer the leaves with cooking spray, and a very light sprinkling of low-fat graham cracker crumbs. Another trick: I spread apricot jam over the bottom of the crust to keep it crispy during baking.

$\mathcal{B}$aked Alaska

MAKES 6 SERVINGS

Prep: 20 minutes
Bake: cakes at 350° for 12 to 14 minutes;
Alaskas at 500° for 3 minutes

On one of my early Cruises to Lose, my socks were knocked off by tuxedoed waiters bringing out huge baked Alaskas for each table. Everybody went ga-ga. It's like the magician pulling the rabbit out of the hat—it gets them every time. People just love the combination of a hot dessert and a cold one. Yum! What's so wonderful about my recipe is that these are individual baked Alaskas. Each person gets his or her own, and it's exactly the right portion. No sneaking back for seconds or even thirds.

NUTRIENT VALUE PER SERVING
316 calories   8 g protein
5 g fat (14% fat)   60 g carbohydrate
290 mg sodium   20 mg cholesterol

1 box angel-food cake mix
4 large egg whites
½ teaspoon cream of tartar
½ cup sugar
1 teaspoon vanilla extract
6 well-frozen scoops reduced-fat
   Neapolitan-flavored ice cream
Fresh whole strawberries, for garnish
(optional)

AHEAD OF TIME

1 Preheat oven to 350°. Line two
15 x 10 x 1-inch jelly-roll pans with
parchment paper or foil. Set aside.
Prepare cake mix according to package
directions. Pour batter into each
prepared pan, spreading evenly.

2 Bake one pan at a time on middle oven
rack for 12 to 14 minutes, until top of
cake is crusty and dry. Loosen edges
with spatula and immediately invert
cakes onto wire racks. Cool. Freeze one
cake for other desserts, such as sundaes
with frozen yogurt and fresh fruit.

3 Using biscuit cutter or kitchen shears,
cut out 6 circles, about 3½ inches in
diameter, from the one cake. Remove
scraps.

4 In deep, narrow-based bowl, bring egg
whites to room temperature. Using
electric mixer, beat egg whites with
cream of tartar until soft peaks form.
Continue beating while adding sugar,
1 tablespoon at a time. Beat until stiff
peaks form. Beat in vanilla. Set
meringue aside.

JUST BEFORE SERVING

5 Preheat oven to 500°. Assemble
Alaskas: Center frozen scoop of ice
cream on each angel-food cake base.
There should be ½ inch of cake border
around base of ice cream.

6 Spoon meringue over each portion of
ice cream, dividing evenly. Working
quickly, use spatula to completely
enclose ice cream with meringue. Be
careful to seal all edges. Meringue
should be about ½ inch thick to meet
with edge of cake. Swirl peaks on top.
Use wide spatula to carefully lift and
place Alaskas a few inches apart on
large baking sheet.

7 Bake 3 minutes or until meringue
is lightly browned. Garnish with
strawberries, if desired. Serve
immediately.

Before Alaska

A dinner guest at the White House in 1802 described an
ice cream dessert that may have been the first public
appearance of baked Alaska. President Jefferson was up
to his old culinary tricks again. As chefs began to play
with this hot and cold dessert, early variations were
actually called Alaska-Florida (hot and cold, get it?). And
then in the late 1800s the dessert appeared on the menu
at Delmonico's, a famous New York City restaurant, and
that really clinched its place on the American table.

So Fine Key Lime Pie

MAKES 10 SERVINGS

Prep: 30 minutes
Chill: 3 hours
Bake: 275° for 40 minutes

One slice of this and you may become a "kissing bandit"—all that pucker power from the lime juice. If you don't happen to be in Key West to find the limes, use bottled lime juice as a substitute.

Snacks for Days

This recipe makes 50 mini-meringues, from one egg white—count them! And you only need about 10 for the pie. Great! You can eat all the rest. Yes, but not all at once. Store them in an airtight container on the counter, and have *one* for a no-fat snack, now and then. Notice I said *one*. All right, *two*.

NUTRIENT VALUE PER SERVING
OF PIE
218 calories   6 g protein
7 g fat (27% fat)   34 g carbohydrate
175 mg sodium   43 mg cholesterol

NUTRIENT VALUE PER MERINGUE
4 calories   0 g protein
0 g fat (0% fat)   1 g carbohydrate
4 mg sodium   0 mg cholesterol

KEY LIME PIE

 2 teaspoons unflavored gelatin
 ½ cup bottled Rose's lime juice
 1 whole large egg
 1 large egg yolk (reserve white to make meringue, see below)
 1 can (14 ounces) fat-free sweetened condensed milk
 ¼ cup evaporated skim milk, well chilled
 1 teaspoon grated lime zest (optional)
 Crumb Pie Crust (recipe opposite page) *or* one 9-inch ready-prepared reduced-fat graham cracker crust
 10 miniature meringues (optional, recipe below)
 10 extra-thin fresh lime slices

MINIATURE MERINGUES

 1 large egg white
 Pinch of salt
 4 tablespoons sugar
 ¼ teaspoon vanilla extract

1 Pie: In small bowl sprinkle gelatin over lime juice. Let stand until softened, 5 minutes. Stir to dissolve gelatin.

2 In large heat-resistant bowl beat whole egg and yolk with electric mixer until thick and lemon colored, about 5 minutes. Add gelatin mixture and condensed milk. Beat on low speed just to mix.

3 In medium saucepan bring 2 cups water to simmer over medium-high heat. Place bowl with egg mixture over saucepan, making sure water does not touch bottom of bowl. Stir egg mixture over simmering water until heated through and thickened, about 10 minutes. Do not let egg mixture boil.

4 Remove bowl from over saucepan. Cool mixture in bowl. Refrigerate just until mixture begins to set. Beat again with mixer at high speed until light and creamy.

5 In small bowl, beat chilled evaporated skim milk with electric mixer until double in volume. Fold into gelatin mixture with lime zest, if using, until thoroughly combined.

6 Pour mixture into pie crust. Refrigerate until set.

7 Meringues: Preheat oven to 275°. Cover baking sheet with wax paper or parchment paper. In medium bowl beat egg white and salt until stiff peaks form. Beat in 3 tablespoons of the sugar gradually until very stiff. Fold in remaining tablespoon sugar and vanilla.

8 Spoon meringue mixture into a sealable plastic bag. Seal. Snip about ¼ inch diagonally from one bottom corner. Squeeze bag gently over prepared baking sheet to force out small dollops of meringue, ¾ inch in diameter. Make dollops until mixture is all used.

9 Bake meringues 40 minutes until dry to touch and lightly colored. With spatula, lift meringues from paper while still warm. Store in airtight container at room temperature or freeze tightly in sealed freezer bag. Use as desired.

10 To serve, arrange lime slices around pie. Top each lime slice with a meringue.

Crumb Pie Crust

In a small bowl or food processor, thoroughly mix 1 cup low-fat graham-cracker crumbs and ¼ teaspoon ground cinnamon. Mix in 3 tablespoons softened light butter until well incorporated. Coat 9-inch pie plate with nonstick butter-flavored cooking spray. Press crumb mixture over bottom and up side of plate. Bake in 375° oven for about 8 minutes or until firm and lightly colored.

Star Strawberry Shortcake

Prep: 15 minutes
Stand: 2 hours
Bake: 450° for 12 to 14 minutes

You've heard of shortcakes and long cakes? Well, this is a star cake—and I guarantee it will make you a culinary hit. Most strawberry shortcakes are piles and piles of whipped cream, and cake, and berries—a flashy showgirl! But take a look at the picture on the opposite page—just a star. Bring this dessert to the dinner table, dipping and swaying with a graceful two-step, humming, *When you wish upon a star . . . .*

2 pints fresh strawberries, hulled and sliced
1 tablespoon granulated sugar

CREAMY TOPPING
1 cup fat-free sour cream
$\frac{1}{2}$ teaspoon vanilla extract
2 tablespoons (packed) light brown sugar

BISCUITS
1$\frac{1}{2}$ cups all-purpose flour, or more as needed
1 tablespoon baking powder
$\frac{1}{4}$ cup granulated sugar
$\frac{1}{4}$ teaspoon salt
$\frac{1}{4}$ cup ($\frac{1}{2}$ stick) chilled light butter, cut into small cubes
$\frac{3}{4}$ cup evaporated skim milk
1 teaspoon grated orange zest

2 teaspoons confectioners' sugar, for garnish (optional)

1 In medium bowl combine strawberries and sugar. Let stand at room temperature about 2 hours, stirring occasionally.

2 Topping: In small bowl whisk together sour cream, vanilla, and brown sugar. Cover and refrigerate.

3 Preheat oven to 450°.

4 Biscuits: In large bowl mix together dry ingredients. Using pastry blender or two knives used like scissors, cut in butter until mixture is coarsely crumbed.

5 Make a well in center. Slowly pour evaporated skim milk and orange zest into well. Toss gently with fork

NUTRIENT VALUE PER SERVING
236 calories   7 g protein
4 g fat (14% fat)   41 g carbohydrate
293 mg sodium   8 mg cholesterol

until soft dough forms. Turn out onto well-floured surface. With floured hands, knead very gently 4 or 5 times. Dough will be wet. Lightly knead in more flour if too wet or loose.

6   Roll out dough or lightly pat to ½-inch thickness. Dip small biscuit cutter—1½-inch round or heart- or star-shaped—into flour, and use to cut biscuits. Use straight motion. Do not twist cutter. Dip cutter into flour between cuts. Lightly gather scraps together as needed to cut out a total of 8 biscuits. Place biscuits close together, but not touching, on baking sheet.

7   Bake 12 to 14 minutes or until biscuits have risen and are golden brown. Transfer biscuits to wire rack to cool a bit.

8   While biscuits are still warm, pull apart or cut in half. Place a biscuit half on each of eight dessert plates. Spoon about ¼ cup of strawberries over each biscuit. Cover with biscuit top. Spoon another ¼ cup of berries over top, plus 2 tablespoons of chilled topping. Dust with sieved confectioners' sugar, if desired. Serve immediately.

Better than Sunshine: Eight medium strawberries = 140 percent of the recommended daily allowance of vitamin C (better than an orange!), and lots of potassium.

Strawberry Festival

Before 1880, when railroads didn't yet carry produce from one coast to another, strawberries were a luxury crop, grown locally by people in their own gardens, or gathered in the wild. Now California grows about 55 percent of the country's commercial supply. For a food festival in the grand old tradition, dress up as a strawberry and visit the June strawberry festival at the United Methodist Church in Ipswich, Massachusetts. There's every imaginable strawberry dish, but you can guess what the star is—you're right, the strawberry shortcake.

Sultry Summer Flan

MAKES 4 SERVINGS

Prep: 15 minutes
Bake: 350° for 35 to 45 minutes

With its Spanish heritage, flan does a perfect olé with the spicy foods of the Southwest. I tried to think of an unusual way to garnish this dessert, but finally decided that some things are best just left alone. A few berries—that's it.

NUTRIENT VALUE PER SERVING
142 calories   10 g protein
trace of fat (1% fat)   24 g carbohydrate
195 mg sodium   3 mg cholesterol

¼ cup sugar

½ cup liquid egg replacement *or* 2 large eggs

Pinch of salt

1 can (12 ounces) evaporated skim milk

1 teaspoon vanilla extract

¼ teaspoon ground nutmeg *or* ground cinnamon

Raspberries, for garnish (optional)

1 Preheat oven to 350°. In small nonstick skillet heat 2 tablespoons sugar over medium-high heat (see Note at right). When sugar starts to melt, reduce heat to medium. Continue to cook sugar, stirring and shaking pan occasionally. When sugar has caramelized (turned medium brown), divide it equally over the bottoms of four 6-ounce soufflé dishes or custard cups. Set aside to cool.

2 In medium bowl whisk egg substitute or whole eggs to combine without making foam. Add salt and remaining sugar. Whisk to mix. Stir in milk, vanilla, and spice.

3 Divide custard over cooled sugar in soufflé dishes. Place dishes in small baking pan. Place pan in oven. Pour enough hot water into baking pan to come halfway up sides of dishes.

4 Bake for 35 to 45 minutes or until knife inserted just off center of flan comes out clean (flans should still be slightly loose and jiggly in center).

5 Serve in soufflé dishes or unmold onto serving plates. Garnish with raspberries, if desired.

Note: To caramelize sugar in microwave oven, divide 2 tablespoons sugar among soufflé dishes. Add 1 teaspoon water to each. Stir to dissolve sugar. Place in microwave oven on HIGH (100% power) for 2 to 3 minutes. Watch carefully and remove cups as soon as sugar turns medium brown.

To Be a Whole Egg, or Not to Be?

I love choices. In this recipe you can go real low-fat with egg substitute, or you can choose a Sacred Fat—whole eggs. It's your choice. Either way, the result is smooth and creamy. Another low-fat secret? I replace the usual heavy cream with evaporated skim milk.

Apricot Bread Pudding

MAKES 4 SERVINGS

Prep: 10 minutes
Stand: 30 minutes
Bake: 350° for 1 hour

This is one of those smiley foods—a comfort dish that makes me feel all good inside. Cookbooks from the late 1700s on are full of recipes for this favorite comfort food. And then in the early 1980s there was the whole rediscovery of bread pudding—it appeared on restaurant menus everywhere— with such bizarre additions as pomegranate seeds and M & Ms. This is a basic version, but with a little flavor trick: I spread the bread with an apricot fruit spread (sugar-free, thank you!) for a sweet-tartness. But you could use any flavor: raspberry, orange, whatever.

Nonstick butter-flavored cooking spray
⅓ to ½ cup sugar-free apricot fruit spread
6 slices French bread (½ inch thick)
1 cup liquid egg substitute
1 can (12 ounces) evaporated skim milk
¼ cup (packed) light brown sugar
1 teaspoon vanilla extract

1 Coat 1½-quart casserole with cooking spray. Spread apricot fruit spread jam evenly over one side of bread slices. Cut into pieces about 1 inch square. Layer bread cubes, spread side up, in casserole.

2 In large bowl whisk egg substitute until light and fluffy. Whisk in milk, sugar, and vanilla. Pour into prepared casserole. Let stand about 30 minutes.

3 Preheat oven to 350°. Bake 1 hour or until knife inserted near center of pudding comes out clean. Pudding should be risen and dry on top.

How to Serve

Did I mention, this is good warm or cold. But please, no bread pudding for breakfast—that's where you'll get in trouble, even though it's low-fat.

NUTRIENT VALUE PER SERVING
324 calories   16 g protein
1 g fat (4% fat)   60 g carbohydrate
376 mg sodium   3 mg cholesterol

Need a Topping?

A dollop of the Creamy Topping from my Thirteen
Colonies Gingerbread (page 182) is delicious on this. Or
puree berries—strawberries, raspberries, or blackberries
(you may want to strain the seeds out, since they can ruin
a smile)—add a splash of orange- or berry-flavored
liqueur if you want to be daring, and you have a quick,
easy, fat-free topping.

Low-Fat Tricks

No heavy cream or egg yolks here, although it tastes like
it. Instead—evaporated skim milk and egg substitute.

$\mathcal{T}$hirteen Colonies Gingerbread

MAKES 12 SERVINGS

Prep: 15 minutes
Bake: 350° for 25 to 45 minutes,
depending on pan size

Once upon a time in the 1300s, before the invention of Parker House rolls, monks served baskets of gingerbread with their monastery meals (so I include some Sacred Fat — light butter — in the recipe). In the 1700s with the addition of molasses, gingerbread traveled the freedom trail to American dessertdom. But big trouble! Molasses, along with tea, was taxed by the British. And we all know what happened after that!

NUTRIENT VALUE PER SERVING
OF PLAIN GINGERBREAD
161 calories   3 g protein
4 g fat (21% fat)   29 g carbohydrate
86 mg sodium   0 mg cholesterol

NUTRIENT VALUE PER
TABLESPOON CREAMY TOPPING
20 calories   1 g protein
0 g fat (0% fat)   4 g carbohydrate
12 mg sodium   0 mg cholesterol

Nonstick butter-flavored cooking spray
¼ cup (½ stick) light butter
½ cup boiling water
½ cup (packed) light brown sugar
½ cup mild molasses
¼ cup liquid egg substitute
1 tablespoon finely grated fresh ginger
1 teaspoon grated lemon zest
1¾ cups all-purpose flour
1 teaspoon baking soda
½ teaspoon ground cinnamon
¼ teaspoon grated nutmeg
⅛ teaspoon ground cloves

CREAMY TOPPING (OPTIONAL)
1 cup fat-free sour cream
½ teaspoon vanilla
2 tablespoons (packed) light brown sugar

Confectioners' sugar, for garnish
1½ cups unsweetened applesauce

1 Preheat oven to 350°. Coat 10-inch tube or Bundt pan (9 to10 cups), or 8-inch round cake pan with cooking spray.

2 Cut butter into small cubes. Place in medium bowl. Pour boiling water over butter. Stir until butter dissolves. Whisk in brown sugar, molasses, egg substitute, ginger, and lemon zest until well mixed.

3 Sift together flour, baking soda, cinnamon, nutmeg, and cloves over butter mixture. Whisk until mixed. Pour batter into prepared pan.

4 Bake 25 to 35 minutes for 10-inch tube or Bundt pan, or 35 to 45 minutes for 8-inch round cake pan, or until wooden pick inserted in center of gingerbread comes out clean.

5 Meanwhile, make Creamy Topping if using. In small bowl whisk together sour cream, vanilla, and brown sugar until smooth. Refrigerate.

6 When gingerbread is done, remove from oven. Cool in pan on wire rack 5 minutes. Turn out onto serving platter.

7 Dust with confectioners' sugar. Serve warm with applesauce and Creamy Topping, if desired.

Dessert Topping

My Creamy Topping, fat-free of course, is good spooned over cut-up fresh fruit, toasted reduced-fat pound cake, or any other dessert where a luscious sauce makes sense.

Red-White-and-Blue Coffeecake

MAKES 16 SERVINGS

Prep: 20 minutes
Bake: 375° for 50 minutes

This is my "Proud to Be an American" cake—the colors of the flag. A great dessert for summer picnics, and really spectacular for a brunch. I dedicate this cake to Neil Diamond and the memory of Kate Smith.

Nonstick butter-flavored cooking spray

CRUMBLY TOPPING
- ¼ cup all-purpose flour
- 2 tablespoons (packed) light brown sugar
- ½ teaspoon ground cinnamon
- 1 tablespoon light butter

CAKE
- 2 cups all-purpose flour
- ¾ cup granulated sugar
- 2 teaspoons baking powder
- ¼ teaspoon salt
- ¾ cup skim milk
- ¼ cup *each* liquid egg substitute *and* light butter, melted
- 1 teaspoon vanilla extract
- 1 cup *each* blueberries *and* cranberries *or* 2 cups blueberries

1 Preheat oven to 375°. Coat 9 x 9 x 2-inch baking pan with cooking spray.

2 Topping: In small bowl combine flour, brown sugar, and cinnamon. With fingertips or two knives used like scissors, cut in butter until mixture is crumbly.

3 Cake: In large bowl combine flour, granulated sugar, baking powder, and salt.

4 In 2-cup liquid measure combine milk, egg substitute, melted butter, and vanilla. Add liquid ingredients to flour mixture. Using electric mixer, beat together

NUTRIENT VALUE PER SERVING
149 calories   3 g protein
4 g fat (21% fat)   27 g carbohydrate
130 mg sodium   0 mg cholesterol

Want to Know More About Cranberries?

This crimson fella was waiting for the Pilgrims when they landed on Cape Cod. And now, every year in South Carver, Massachusetts, there's a Cranberry Festival, and just a short drive away in Plymouth you can visit the "rock" and the Cranberry World museum—and become a cranberry expert.

about 30 seconds. Fold in berries. Pour batter into prepared pan. Cover batter evenly with topping mixture.

5 Bake 50 minutes or until wooden pick inserted in center of cake comes out clean. Best served warm, but also delicious cold.

Make-a-Date Spicy Fruit Loaf

Prep: 20 minutes
Bake: 350° for 1 hour

I first tasted a version of this at the National Date Festival in Indio, California. It was good. I took some home and it just got better the second and third days. The spices mellowed, the dried fruit made the loaf sweeter-tasting — it's all those things that have happened to *me* over the years! I love a slice of this for breakfast or with a cup of herbal tea in the afternoon. I've even been known to spread a little reduced-fat cream cheese on a slice.

Nonstick vegetable oil cooking spray
1 cup chopped mixed dried fruit
1 tablespoon *plus* ¾ cup all-purpose flour
¾ cup whole-wheat flour
1 tablespoon baking powder
2 teaspoons ground cinnamon
¼ teaspoon *each* ground cloves *and* ground nutmeg *and* ground ginger *and* salt
⅔ cup (packed) light brown sugar
1½ cups bran flakes–style cereal
4 large egg whites
1 packet butter-flavored granules mixed with ½ cup hot water *or* ½ cup low-fat buttermilk
¾ cup skim milk

1 Preheat oven to 350°. Coat 9 x 5 x 3-inch nonstick loaf pan with cooking spray.

2 In small bowl toss dried fruit with 1 tablespoon all-purpose flour.

3 Into large bowl stir together ¾ cup all-purpose flour, whole-wheat flour, baking powder, cinnamon, cloves, nutmeg, ginger, and salt. Add sugar and cereal.

4 In large bowl beat egg whites until foamy. Stir in liquefied butter-flavored granules or buttermilk, and skim milk.

5 Stir liquid ingredients into flour mixture until just moistened. Fold in dried fruit. Scrape mixture into prepared pan.

NUTRIENT VALUE PER SERVING
119 calories   3 g protein
trace of fat (2% fat)   27 g carbohydrate
174 mg sodium   0 mg cholesterol

6 Bake 1 hour or until wooden pick inserted in center of loaf comes out clean. Cool in pan on wire rack for 15 minutes. Remove from pan and cool on rack completely.

Get Out the Fat!

This recipe has practically no fat—not true with the date loaf I first had in Indio. No whole eggs, just whites. And I use butter-flavored granules to make it taste richly fatty, but without fat. I discovered that low-fat buttermilk has the same effect. And you know what else I sneaked into this recipe? Whole-wheat flour and bran cereal for extra vitamins and minerals. Who would have thought!

Index